FIRST LESSONS

IN

SANSKRIT GRAMMAR

FIRST LESSONS

IN

SANSKRIT GRAMMAR,

TOGETHER WITH

AN INTRODUCTION TO THE

HITOPADESA.

BY

JAMES R. BALLANTYNE, LL.D.

GYAN

Published by

Gyan Publishing House
5, Ansari Road
Daryaganj, New Delhi-110002
Phone: 011-47034999, 9811692060
E-mail: books@gyanbooks.com

Distribution Network
gyanbooks.com
India, USA, Canada, UK, Australia

ISBN: 978-93-6208-182-7 (PB)
First Published, 1851

2nd Impression 2024

Printed at: Gyan Press, Delhi.

FIRST LESSONS IN SANSKRIT GRAMMAR
Author: JAMES R. BALLANTYNE

FIRST LESSONS

IN

SANSKRIT GRAMMAR

TOGETHER WITH

AN INTRODUCTION TO THE

HITOPADEŚA.

BY

JAMES R. BALLANTYNE, LL.D.

LIBRARIAN OF THE INDIA OFFICE.

FIFTH EDITION.

LONDON:

KEGAN PAUL, TRENCH, TRÜBNER, & CO. LTD

PATERNOSTER HOUSE, CHARING CROSS ROAD.

1892.

ADVERTISEMENT TO THE SECOND EDITION.

The little brochure which, as above indicated, I prepared, some eleven years ago, for the use of my English pupils in the Benares College, has met with unexpected favour in England. At the instigation of teachers and publishers, I reprint it, with the addition of "An Introduction to the *Hitopadeśa*", the design of which Introduction is stated at page 47 of the present volume. I make a present of the edition to my worthy publisher, and I trust he will not suffer by accepting the risk of its publication. With a view to diminishing that risk, it may be as well to anticipate a possible (or actual) question or two.

"Can a book of this kind,"—It may be asked,—"prepared for Hindús, be a quite suitable book for learners in England?" I answer —"Yes:—if suitable for the one class, it is suitable for the other." The mere students of English, in the Government Colleges in India, have lost—as the bulk of English boys are not now required to have— the power (—so remarkable in Hindú children—) of learning by heart long strings of words and long strings of rules, not merely without explanation—but—without repugnance. The Hindú student who has devoted himself (—as so many now do—) to the nearly exclusive study of English,—and, on the other hand, the English youth, stand therefore in much the same position as regards their entrance on the study of Sanskrit.

"But are these 'First Lessons' not intended to seduce the learner into the study of the *Kaumudí*, and of the *Páṇiníya* grammatical system generally?" I reply by quoting, from the above Advertisement to the First Edition, my anticipation that he who should have gone through this introduction would not "be so readily repelled by a grammar which starts from the driest elements of the subject,—like the grammars of Professors Wilson and Williams".

"But are all the exercises in these 'First Lessons',—particularly the exercises for translation from English into Sanskrit,—of progressive difficulty,—like those in the 'Sanskrit Manual' just published by the Boden Professor of Sanskrit?" I reply,—"Not so,—and intentionally not so." The Advertisement to the First Edition shows, I think, with sufficient plainness, that my design is to tempt the student *to enter on the subject*,—to lure him on to a Pisgah-prospect of the Land of Promise, —and then to let him buckle manfully to the struggle if the prospect tempt him. This is a much humbler aim than that of the Boden Professor's "Sanskrit Manual"; but it is one which may, perhaps, not unadvisably precede it. How many persons, who would have been repelled by Archbishop Whately's "Synthetical Compendium" of Logic, have been conciliated to the study by his delightful "Analytical Outline"! To the mere beginner it is *not*, in my opinion, advantageous that each successive step should be a harder step, and more uphill,—as Milo's bull-calf proved heavier every day he carried him. The sixth Proposition of Euclid's "First Book" is a positively salutary relief after the pains and perils of the "Pons Asinorum". A journey *all* uphill is less pleasant than one with alternations of ascent, descent, and occasional level; and further, it is not only less pleasant, but less profitable, to him whom the first hard climb provokes to turn back in disgust.

In the preparation of the original brochure I was pleasantly aided by my coadjutor in the then recently established Anglo-Sanskrit department of the Benares College—Professor Fitz-Edward Hall, D.C.L., Oxon.—who, being amused by the plan of the work, took a lively interest in its preparation. If this extended edition had undergone his critical revision, I should feel more confidence in its faultlessness;—but, such as it is, Dr. Hall will not, I hope, disdain this dedication of it to him, as a memento of our joint labours, in happy bygone years, at Benares.

J. R. B.

INDIA-OFFICE LIBRARY
5th February 1862.

ADVERTISEMENT TO THE FIRST EDITION.

THE opinion has been adopted by the Government of the N. W. Provinces that the study of Sanskrit, by the English pupils in the Government Colleges, might be made to furnish a means of mental discipline analogous to that which the study of the Latin and the Greek furnishes in Europe.

In these "First Lessons", the plan of which was suggested by Mr. T. K. Arnold's "First Latin Book", and which are intended to precede the study of any regular Sanskrit grammar, the etymological rules for the permutation of letters in the formation of words, which in the regular grammars the learner encounters at the outset, are remitted to a later division of the work,—attention being called at the outset to those syntactical rules only—and to each rule only when a special occasion for it arises—which are of constant application in modifying the appearance of perfect words when they come together in a sentence.

Attention is also confined, in the first instance, to those forms, (such as the 3d person singular of the verb) in which the most constantly recurring words present themselves in sentences, and the pupil is set at once to write exercises, in which a number of useful words are repeated so frequently as to render unlikely their being readily forgotten again. The pupil, whilst making progress, will here probably have the pleasant feeling that he is making progress:—and, after mastering this introduction, he will not be so readily repelled by a grammar which starts from the driest elements of the subject,—like the grammars of Professors Wilson and Williams, or the *Laghu Kaumudí*, with its English Version.

If it should be thought that too little demand is here made upon the learner for the exertion of mental effort—the reply is this, that the main purpose of these exercises is not so much to provoke mental effort as to imprint on the memory of the learner some of the broadest outlines of a subject which, first presented in all its details, is apt to prove repulsively bewildering.

J. R. B.

BENARES COLLEGE, 1850.
8th September.

INDEX.

PART I.

PART II

CHAPTER I.

CHAPTER II.

CHAPTER III.

CHAPTER IV

INTRODUCTION.

THE DEVANÁGARÍ ALPHABET.

VOWELS, &c.

अ *a*, आ *á*, इ *i*, ई *í*, उ *u*, ऊ *ú*, ऋ *ṟi*, ॠ *ṟí*, ऌ *lṟi*, ॡ *lṟí*
ए *e*, ऐ *ai*, ओ *o*, औ *au*. ं (*anuswára*) *ṅ*, ः (*visarga*) *ḥ*.

CONSONANTS.

Gutturals	क *ka*,	ख *kha*,	ग *ga*,	घ *gha*,	ङ *ṅa*,
Palatals	च *cha*,	छ *chha*,	ज *ja*,	झ *jha*,	ञ *ña*.
Cerebrals.	ट *ṭa*,	ठ *ṭha*,	ड *ḍa*,	ढ *ḍha*,	ण *ṉa*.
Dentals.	त *ta*,	थ *tha*	द *da*,	ध *dha*,	न *na*.
Labials.	प *pa*,	फ *pha*,	ब *ba*,	भ *bha*,	म *ma*,
Semi-vowels.	य *ya*,	र *ra*,	ल *la*,	व *va*, or *wa*.	
Sibilants and Aspirate	श *śa*,	ष *sha*,	स *sa*,	ह *ha*.	

The vowels in the foregoing scheme, as throughout the following pages, must be pronounced as follows: viz. *a* as in *Roman;* *á* as in *father;* *i* as in *it;* *í* as in *police;* *u* as in *push;* *ú* as in *rude;* *e* as in *there;* *ai* as in *aisle;* *o* as in *so;* *au* as *ow* in *now.* The consonants are, in general, pronounced as in English. But *th* and *ph* must be sounded as in the words *anthill* and *uphill,* not as in *this* and *philology.*

The above forms of the *vowels* are used only at the beginning of a syllable. The vowel अ *a* is inherent in every consonant, and is sounded after every one which has not the mark of a pause thus—(viz. ्) subscribed, nor another vowel, in a contracted shape, attached to it. These other vowels, when not at the beginning of a syllable, assume the following contracted shapes.

MEDIAL AND FINAL FORMS OF THE VOWELS.

ा *á*, ि *i*, ी *í*, ु *u*, ू *ú*, ृ *ṛi*, ॄ *ṛí*, ॢ *ḷṛi*, ॣ *ḷṛí*, े *e*, ै *ai*, ो *o*, ौ *au*.

Examples of the Vowels following the letter क् *k*.

क *ka*, का *ká*, कि *ki*, की *kí*, कु *ku*, कू *kú*, कृ *kṛi*, कॄ *kṛí*, कॢ *klṛi*, कॣ *klṛí*, के *ke*, कै *kai*, को *ko*, कौ *kau*, कं *kaṅ*, or *kam*, कः *kah*. The vowels *u* and *ú* are added to the letter र् *r* thus—रु *ru*, रू *rú*.

When two or more consonants meet, without the intervention of a vowel, they coalesce and become one conjunct character. These compounds are formed by writing the subsequent consonant under the first, by blending them in a particular way, or by writing them in their usual order, omitting the perpendicular stroke of each letter except the last.

The letter र् *r*, when it immediately precedes a consonant, is written above it, in the form of a crescent, thus, र्ग *rga*: when it immediately follows one, it is written as a slanting line beneath it thus, क्र *kra*, ग्र *gra*.

The following are among the most frequently recurring of the

CONJUNCT CONSONANTS.

क्त *kta*, क्व *kwa*, क्त्व *ktwa*, क्ष *ksha*, क्ष्य *kshya*, क्ष्व *kshwa*, ख्य *khya*, ग्र *gra*, ग्र्य *grya*, घ्न *ghna*, ङ्क *ṅka*, ङ्ग *ṅga*, च्च *chcha*, च्छ *chchha*, ज्ज *jja*, ज्ञ *jña*,* ज्य *jya*, ज्र *jra*, ञ्च *ñcha*, ण्ट *ṇṭa*, त्त *tta*, त्न *tna*, त्र *tra*, त्र्य *trya*, त्व *twa*, द्द *dda*, द्ध *ddha*, द्भ *dbha*, द्भ्य *dbhya*, द्य *dya*, द्र *dra*, ध्व *dhwa*, न्त्य *ntya*, न्त्र *ntra*, प्त *pta*, भ्य *bhya*, श्च *ścha*, श्र *śra*, श्व *śwa*, ष्ट *shṭa*, ष्य *shya*, स्त *sta*, स्त्र *stra*, स्थ *stha*, स्य *sya*, ह्ण *hṇa*, ह्न *hna*, ह्म *hma*, ह्य *hya*, ह्र *hra*,

* Commonly pronounced *gya*.

Lesson I.

1.—A Sanskrit noun, as it stands in the dictionary, is said to be in the *crude form.*

2.—Nouns, in the crude form, end either in a vowel or in a consonant.

3.—The vowels with which most nouns end are अ *a*, आ *á*, इ *i*, ई *í*, उ *u*, and ऋ *ṛi*.

4. Nouns are *Masculine*, *Feminine*, and *Neuter*. Names of males are masculine, and those of females feminine; but many words are masculine or feminine, which are names neither of males nor of females. For example, रथ *ratha*, 'a car,' is masculine; and चिन्ता *chintá*, 'reflection,' is feminine. Those that end in *ā* or *ī* are generally feminine.

5.—By adding to, or otherwise changing, the crude form of the noun, seven different forms, with different senses, are obtained. These altered forms are called *cases*.

6.—The 1st case is that in which a noun appears when it denotes the *subject* spoken of in the sentence. This case is called the *Subjective*, or, more commonly, the *Nominative* case.

7.—Words which, in the *crude form*, end in the vowels set down in No. 3, commonly make the Nominative by altering the terminations thus:—

अ *a* becomes, in the Nominative, अः *ah*.

आ *ā*, remains unaltered.

इ *i*	becomes, in the Nominative,		इः *ih*.
ई *í*	....	....	ईः *íh*.
उ *u*	....	....	उः *uh*.
ऋ *ṛi*	....	....	आ *á*.

N. B.—*Neuter* nouns ending in अ *a* make the Nominative in अं *am*.

Exercise 1.

8.—Write down the Nominative case of each of the following words both in Devanágarí and English characters.

VOCABULARY 1.

अश्व *aśwa,* a horse.

इच्छा *ichchhá,* wish.

आसन *ásana* (n.*), a seat.

वीणा *víṇa,* a lute.

बुद्धि *buddhi,* understanding.

गुरु *guru,* a preceptor.

अग्नि *agni,* fire.

काक *káka,* a crow.

माला *málá,* a garland.

श्री *śrí,* prosperity.

गुण *guṇa,* a quality.

पितृ *pitṛi,* a father.

वचन *vachana* (n.), speech.

चन्द्र *chandra,* the moon.

देव *deva,* a god.

पूजा *pújá,* worship.

गृह *gṛiha* (n.), a house.

धर्म्म *dharmma,* merit.

वन *vana* (n.), a wood.

मातृ *mátṛi,* a mother.

पर्व्वत *parvvata,* a mountain.

मध्य *madhya,* the midst.

हिंसा *hiṁsá,* injury.

पत्र *patra* (n.), a leaf.

पति *pati,* a master.

धातृ *dhátṛi,* a creator.

पान्थ *pántha,* a traveller.

जल *jala* (n.), water.

फल *phala* (n.), fruit.

रावण *rávaṇa,* Rávaṇa.

वृक्ष *vṛiksha,* a tree.

बक *baka,* a crane.

दुःख *du'kha* (n.), pain.

शत्रु *śatru,* an enemy.

सभा *sabhá,* an assembly.

कर्त्तृ *karttṛi,* a doer.

शिष्य *śishya,* a disciple.

शृगाल *śṛigála,* a jackall.

कुल *kula* (n.), a family.

दुहितृ *duhitṛi,* a daughter.

समुद्र *samudra,* the ocean.

पुस्तक *pustaka* (n.), a book.

कन्या *kanyá,* a girl.

व्याघ्र *vyághra,* a tiger.

दातृ *dátṛi,* a giver.

हस्त *hasta,* the hand.

राम *ráma,* Ráma.

शास्त्र *śástra* (n.), a scripture.

* The letter 'n' indicates that the word is Neuter.

ब्राह्मण *bráhman̲a*, a Bráhman̲.

तीर *tíra* (n.), a shore, or bank.

नर *nara*, a man, or male.

मनुष्य *manushya*, a man.

पुत्र *putra*, a son.

धन *dhana* (n.), wealth.

मृग *mṛiga*, a deer.

अन्न *anna* (n.), food.

हरि *hari*, Vishnu.

क्रोध *krodha*, anger.

बाण *bán̲a*, an arrow.

चक्र *chakra* (n.), a wheel.

मस्तक *mastaka* (n.), the head.

प्रभु *prabhu*, lord.

शक्ति *śakti*, power.

सर्प *sarpa*, a snake.

भक्त *bhakta*, a devotee.

भूमि *bhúmi*, the ground.

कपि *kapi*, a monkey.

हुत *huta* (n.), a sacrifice.

पुष्प *pushpa* (n.), a flower.

कवि *kavi*, a poet.

ग्राम *gráma*, a village.

क्रिया *kriyá*, action.

रुचि *ruchi*, relish.

पातक *pátaka* (n.), sin.

विद्या *vidyá*, knowledge.

मूषिक *múshika*, a mouse.

चौर *chaura*, a thief.

बाल *bála*, a boy.

मालिक *málika*, a gardener.

आराम *áráma*, a garden.

तारा *tárá*, a star.

Lesson 2.

9.—Some final consonants, in the formation of the Nominative case, are changed thus:—

च् *ch* or श् *ś* becomes क् *k*. A final न् *n* is dropped, and the preceding vowel (if the word is not neuter) is lengthened.

र् *r* is changed to *visarga*, and the vowel is lengthened.

10.—An aspirated letter (*e. g.* ख *kha*) is changed to the corresponding unaspirated letter (*e.g.* क *ka*).

11.—Some final consonants undergo no change.

Exercise 2.

12.—Write down the Nominative case of each of the following words in Devanágarí and English characters.

VOCABULARY 2.

वाच् *vách*, a word.	दिश् *diś*, a side, direction.
राजन् *rájan*, a king.	आत्मन् *átman*, soul.
हस्तिन् *hastin*, an elephant.	विद्युत् *vidyut*, lightning.
गिर् *gir*, a word.	नामन् *náman* (n.), a name.
जगत् *jagat*, the world.	चित्रलिख् *chitralikh*, a painter.

Lesson 3.

13.—A Sanskrit verb, as it stands in the dictionary, appears in the form called the *root.*

14.—To make the 3d person singular of the present tense, the syllable ति *ti* is subjoined to the root. Thus, for example, from the root अस् *as*, 'to be,' is formed अस्ति *asti*, 'he is.'

15.—When such a termination as *ti* (No. 14.) is subjoined, the root generally requires to undergo some change. According to the nature of this change, roots are divided into *classes* or *conjugations*, of which there are reckoned *ten.*

16.—Roots of the 1st conjugation interpose the short vowel अ *a* between the final and such a termination as *ti* (No. 14.), and they change a final simple vowel in the root, (or a short vowel when a single consonant follows,) into its corresponding *improper diphthong.*

17.—The *improper diphthongs*, or *guṇa* substitutes for the vowels, are the following:—

Of इ *i* or	ई *í* the	*guṇa*	substitute is	ए	*e.*
— उ *u* or	ऊ *ú*	—	—	ओ	*o.*
— ऋ *ri* or	ॠ *rí*	—	—	अर्	*ar.*

18.—The improper diphthong ए *e* is changed to अय् *ay*, and ओ *o* to अव् *av*, when a vowel follows.

Exercise 3.

19.—Write down the 3d person singular present tense of each of the following verbs of the 1st conjugation, both in Devanágarí and English letters, with the meaning in English.

VOCABULARY 3.

भू *bhú*, to become.
अट् *aṭ*, to rove.
अर्ह् *arh*, to be fit.
क्षि *kshi*, to decay.
चर् *char*, to go, or get along.
जि *ji*, to conquer.
तॄ *tṛí*, to cross over.
त्यज् *tyaj*, to abandon.
दह् *dah*, to burn.
द्रु *dru*, to ooze.
पच् *pach*, to cook.
वद् *vad*, to speak.
वस् *vas*, to dwell.
वह् *vah*, to carry.
शुच् *śuch*, to sorrow for.
श्रि *śri*, to serve.
सृ *sṛi*, to go.
सृप् *sṛip*, to creep.
स्मृ *smṛi*, to remember.
हस् *has*, to laugh.
हृ *hṛi*, to take.
खन् *khan*, to dig.
पत् *pat*, to fall.
फल् *phal*, to bear fruit.
बुध् *budh*, to know.
व्रज् *vraj*, to go.
जल्प् *jalp*, to prate.
चल् *chal*, to move.

भ्रम् *bhram*, to wander.

Example. The root of भू *bhú*, by No. 16, becomes भो *bho*; and the vowel अ *a* is to be interposed between this and the termination ति *ti* (No. 14)—so that we have *bho* + *a* + *ti*;—and then, the *o* being changed to *av* by No. 18—we have भवति *bhavati*, 'he becomes.'

Lesson 4.

20.—When one Sanskrit word immediately follows another,

some change often takes place in the two letters thus brought together.

21.—If the former of two words placed next to each other ends in अः *ah,* and the other begins with a *soft** *consonant,* the अः *ah* is changed to ओ *o*. For example, when देवः *devaḥ,* the nominative singular (No. 8.) of देव *deva,* 'a god,' is placed before वदति *vadati,* the 3d person singular present tense (No. 19) of वद् *vad,* 'to speak'—the two are written thus—देवो वदति *devo vadati,* 'the god speaks.'

See further under Nos. 94 and 95.

Exercise 4.

22.—Write the following phrases in Sanskrit, both in Devanágarí and English letters, taking the words from Vocabularies 1 and 3, and paying attention to the rule—No. 21.

The crane wanders. The Bráhmaṉ cooks. The god laughs. The jackal dwells. The quality becomes. The horse carries. The traveller knows. The tree falls. The man prates. The leaf decays. The daughter abandons. The father crosses over. The mouse digs. The water oozes. The mother speaks. The girl serves. The boy is fit.

23.—Write down the meaning, in English, of the following phrases:—

रामो जयति । शृगालो हरति । रावणो व्रजति । पुत्रः स्मरति । वृक्षः फलति । देवो वदति । नरो बोधति । पत्रं चलति । ब्राह्मणो भ्रमति । मृगो वसति । पान्थो जल्पति । माता हसति ।

Lesson 5.

24.—If the former of two words placed next to each other ends

* The *soft* consonants are *ga, gha ; ja, jha ; ḍa, ḍha ; da, dha ; ba, bha ;* the nasals, the semi-vowels, and *ha.*

in *visarga*, and the other begins with any *hard** *consonant* (except a guttural, a labial, or a sibilant—before which the termination may remain unchanged—) the *visarga* is changed to a *sibilant*. For example, when the word तरति *tarati* comes after the word ब्राह्मणः *bráhman̲ah*, the two are written thus—ब्राह्मणस्तरति *bráhman̲as-tarati*, 'the Bráhman̲ crosses over.'

25.—A sibilant† must be of the same class as the consonant with which it coalesces,—that is to say, श् *ś* is the sibilant when a *palatal*, such as च *cha*, follows; and ष् *sh* when a *cerebral*, such as ट *ṭa* follows.

Exercise 5.

26.—Write down, in Sanskrit, the following phrases, taking the words from Vocabularies 1 and 3.

The devotee crosses over. The tree decays. The Bráhman̲ abandons. The jackal creeps. The son remembers.

27.—Write down the meaning, in English, of the following phrases:—

मृगः सरति । शृगालश्चरति । रामः स्मरति । पुत्रः पचति । अश्वः पतति । रावणस्त्यजति । पान्थश्चरति । नरः श्रयति । वृक्षः क्षयति ।

Lesson 6.

28.—The 2d person singular 2d future ends in स्यति *syati* or इष्यति *ishyati*. Thus the verb भू *bhú*, which makes भवति in the present, makes in the future भविष्यति *bhavishyati*, 'he will become.'

Exercise 6.

29.—Write the following phrases in Sanskrit:—

The horse will fall. The Bráhman̲ will speak. The son will

* The *hard* consonants are *ka*, *kha*; *cha*, *chha*; *ṭa*, *ṭha*; *ta*, *tha*; *pa*, *pha*; and the sibilants.

† श is the palatal sibilant, ष the cerebral, and स the dental.

wander. The tree will bear fruit. The man will remember. The jackal will take. The Bráhmaṉ will know. Ráma will laugh. The horse will go. Rávaṉa will cross over, Ráma will conquer.

30.—When the future is formed by **स्यति** *syati* (No. 28) some change often takes place in the final of the verb. The following list may be committed to memory :—

त्यक्ष्यति *tyakshyati,* 'he will abandon.'
धक्ष्यति *dhakshyati,* 'he will burn.'
द्रोष्यति *droshyati,* 'it will ooze.'
पक्ष्यति *pakshyati,* 'he will cook.'
जेष्यति *jeshyati,* 'he will conquer.'
वत्स्यति *vatsyati,* 'he will dwell.'

Exercise 7.

31.—Write down, in English, the meaning of the following phrases :—

जलं द्रोष्यति । नरः पक्ष्यति । व्याघ्रो जेष्यति । नरो वत्स्यति । चौरस्त्यक्ष्यति । ब्राह्मणो भ्रमिष्यति । देवः स्मरिष्यति । काको हरिष्यति । पिता बोधिष्यति ।

Lesson 7.

32.—The 2d case is that in which a noun appears when it is the *object* of a transitive verb. This case is called the *Objective,* or, more commonly, the *Accusative,* case.

33.—A transitive verb is one which gives no *complete* meaning, till some person or thing is mentioned, as the object *to whom* or *to which* the action was done.

Ráma killed—(killed whom?) Rávaṉa.

34.—The following are the accusative singular endings of nouns that, in the crude form, end in a vowel:—

अ	*a* becomes	अं	*am.*
आ	*á* ——	आं	*ám.*
इ	*i* ——	इं	*im.*
ई	*í* ——	ईं	*ím.*
उ	*u* ——	उं	*um.*

ऋ *ri*—(in some words) अरं *aram*, (in others) आरं *áram.*

35.—The *anuswára*, when followed by a vowel, takes the form of म् *m.* When followed by a consonant of the five classes, the guttural, &c., it optionally takes the form as well as the sound of the nasal belonging to the same class. Otherwise it remains unchanged. Thus अन्नं वहति *annam vahati*, 'he carries the food'—अन्नम्पचति *annam pachati*, 'he cooks the food'—अन्नन्त्यजति *annan tyajati*, 'he abandons the food.'

Observe that the accusative is generally placed before the verb, as in the examples just given.

Exercise 8.

36.—Write down, in English, the meaning of the following phrases:—

अन्नम्पचति नरः। गृहन्त्यजति पुत्रः। शास्त्रं स्मरति ब्राह्मणः। पुत्रो बोधति पितरम्। सभान्त्यजति रावणः। शत्रुं जयति रामः। मातरं स्मरति बालः। हरिं स्मरिष्यति ब्राह्मणः।

Exercise 9.

37.—Put into Sanskrit the following phrases:—

The father knows (his) son. The Bráhman will remember the

scripture. Ráma will abandon the house. The car carries the man. The son will cook the food. The devotee will know the god. The crane will cross the water. The mouse will dig the ground. The son will serve the father.

Lesson 8.

38.—Some useful verbs of the 1st conjugation form the present and some of the other tenses irregularly. The following roots, with their 3d person singular present, may be committed to memory:—

क्रम् *kram* makes क्रामति *krámati*, 'he walks.'
गम् *gam* — गच्छति *gachchhati*, 'he goes.'
गुप् *gup* — गोपायति *gopáyati*, 'he protects.'
घ्रा *ghrá* — जिघ्रति *jighrati*, 'he smells.'
जीव् *jív* — जीवति *jívati*, 'he lives.'
दा *dá* — यच्छति *yachchhati*, 'he gives.'
दृश् *driś* — पश्यति *paśyaṭi*, 'he sees.'
पा *pá* — पिबति *pibati*, 'he drinks.'
ष्ठा *shṭhá* — तिष्ठति *tishṭhati*, 'he stands.'
श्रु *śru* — शृणोति *śṛinoti*, 'he hears.'

39.—When the 3d person singular ends in अति *ati*, the 3d person plural ends in अन्ति *anti*. Thus भवन्ति *bhavanti*, 'they become.'

40.—The *negative* is न *na*, 'not;' as न भवति *na bhavati*, 'he does not become;' न भवन्ति *na bhavanti*, 'they do not become.'

41.—*Interrogatives* are किम् *kim*, 'what?'—कुत्र *kutra*, 'where?'—कदा *kadá*, 'when?'—कुतः *kutah*, 'whence?'—

किमर्थम् *kim-artham*, 'why?'—कथम् *katham*, 'how?' &c. Examples: किं वदति *kim vadati*, 'what does he say?' कुत्र वसति *kutra vasati*, 'where does he dwell?' किमर्थम्पितरम्पुत्रो न स्मरति *kimartham pitaram putro na smarati*, 'why does the son not remember the father?'

42.—Verbs signifying '*to go to*' require the accusative of the place gone to. Ex. काशीं गच्छति *káśín gachchhati*, 'he goes to Káśí (Benares).'

Exercise 10.

43.—The son smells the flower. They go to Káśí. The crow does not see the jackal. Ráma walks to the mountain. Why does not the father protect the son? The Bráhman drinks water. He gives the food. The Bráhman remembers the scripture.

Lesson 9.

44.—The *Nominative plural* is frequently formed by changing the termination as follows:—

अ *a* (masculine) or आ *á* (mas. or fem.) becomes आः *áh*.
अ *a* (neuter) — — आनि *áni*.
इ *i* (mas. or fem.) — — अयः *ayah*.
उ *u* — — — अवः *avah*.
ऋ *ri* — — अरः *arah* or आरः *árah*.

45.—When a soft consonant, or a vowel, comes after आ *áh*, the *visarga* is dropped. Ex. नराः *naráh*, 'men':—नरा वसन्ति *nará vasanti*, 'men dwell:'—नरा अर्हन्ति *nará arhanti*, 'the men are fit.'

Exercise 11.

46.—The mice creep. The thieves take the food. The men laugh. The Bráhmans will prate. The jackals drink water.

When will the sons cook the food? The fathers do not see the flower. The men go to the shore. The Bráhmans will not cross the sea. The flowers fall. What do the men say?

किमर्थं नरा न वदन्ति। वृक्षाः पतिष्यन्ति। अन्नं पुत्राः पश्यन्ति। काकाः कुत्र गच्छन्ति। कन्या तीरं गच्छति। कवयो वदिष्यन्ति। पितरस्तीरं गच्छन्ति। वृक्षाः क्षयन्ति।

Lesson 10.

47.—The *Accusative plural masculine* is formed by changing the termination, as follows:—

अ *a*	becomes	आन् *án.*		इ *i*	becomes	ईन् *ín.*
उ *u*	—	ऊन् *ún.*		ऋ *ri*	—	ॠन् *rín.*

Ex. देवान् स्मरति *deván smarati*, 'he remembers the gods':— शत्रून् पश्यति *śatrún paśyati*, 'he sees the enemies.'

Obs. A neuter word is always the same in the accusative as in the nominative:—thus, (No. 44) पुष्पाणि पश्यति *pushpáni paśyati*, 'he sees the flowers.'

48.—When a soft consonant or a vowel follows, then, इः *ih* becomes इर् *ir;* and, in like manner, ईः *íh* becomes ईर् *ír:* उः *uh* becomes उर् *ur;* एः *eh* becomes एर् *er;* ऐः *aih* becomes ऐर् *air;* ओः *oh* becomes ओर् *or;* and औः *auh* becomes और *aur.* Ex. कविर्वदति *kavir vadati*, 'the poet says.'

Exercise 12.

49.—The crows see the jackals. The jackals do not see the crows. Ráma sees (his) enemies. The sons protect (their) fathers. Why do the sons not protect (their) fathers? Ráma protects the monkeys. The fathers sorrow for (their) sons. The

Bráhmaṇs remember the scriptures. The boy smells the flowers. When do the men go to the villages?

पुत्राः कथं शास्त्राणि स्मरिष्यन्ति । पितॄन् कदा गोपायिष्यन्ति पुत्राः । कुत्र गच्छन्ति शत्रवः । शृगालान् कथं न पश्यन्ति काकाः । अग्निर्वृक्षान् धंक्ष्यति । गृहं गच्छन्ति ब्राह्मणाः । दुहिता पश्यति पितरम् । कविः सभां गच्छति । कुलं स्मरन्ति पितरः । तीरं गमिष्यन्ति बकाः । शत्रून् कुत्र पश्यति रामः । शत्रून् जेष्यति देवः । कुतो धनं हरन्ति चैाराः ।

Lesson 11.

50.—The singular of the 3d, or *Instrumental*, case, is frequently formed by changing the termination as follows :—

अ *a* becomes एन *ena.*		इ *i* becomes इना *iná.*	
उ *u* — उना *uná.*		ऋ *ri* — रा *rá.*	

Ex. हस्तेन हरति *hastena harita,* 'he takes with the hand':— अग्निना दहति *agniná dahati,* 'he burns with fire.'

Exercise 13.

51.—The men cook the food with fire. The Bráhmaṇ burns the sacrifice with fire. The son, with his hand, carries the flower. Rávaṇa, with anger, sees the enemies. When does Rávaṇa see the enemies with anger? When will the man take the flower with his hand? How will the deer cross over the water? The son, by wealth, protects (his) father. Men live by food.

Lesson 12.

52.—The *indefinite past participle passive* generally ends in त *ta,* and, like an adjective in अ *a,* takes the three genders, thus :—

	Masculine.	*Feminine.*	*Neuter.*
Sing. nom.	तः *tah.*	ता *tá.*	तम् *tam.*

53.—The following list of past participles may be committed to memory:—

स्मृत	*smṛita,*	'remembered.'
उक्त	*ukta,*	'said, or spoken.'
त्यक्त	*tyakta,*	'abandoned.'
हृत	*hṛita,*	'taken.'
जित	*jita,*	'conquered.'
गत	*gata,*	'gone.'
दत्त	*datta,*	'given.'
दृष्ट	*dṛishṭa,*	'seen.'
पतित	*patita,*	'fallen.'
पीत	*píta,*	'drunk.'
यत	*yata,*	'restrained.'
जात	*játa,*	'born, produced.'
भूत	*bhúta,*	'been.'
श्रुत	*śruta,*	'heard.'

Exercise 14.

54.—Translate the following phrases:—

शास्त्रं ब्राह्मणेन स्मृतम् । पुत्रः पित्रा त्यक्तः । अन्नं हस्तेन हृतम् । रावणो रामेण जितः । नरो ग्रामं गतः । कन्या पित्रा दत्ता । धनं चौरेण हृष्टम् । जलं ब्राह्मणेन पीतम् । क्रोधो भक्तेन जितः ।

The son, abandoned by his father, goes to the village. Rávaṇa, conquered by Ráma, will fall. The jackal, seen by the man, will abandon the village. The sons, abandoned by the father, will wander. The crow, seen by the jackal, drinks water.

Lesson 13.

55.—The 2d preterite is distinguished by the reduplication of the root. The termination of the 3d person singular is अ *a*; but if the root ends in आ *á*, the termination is औ *au.*

56.—In the reduplication of the root, a guttural is changed to a palatal—*e.g.* क् *k* or ख् *kh* is changed to च् *ch*; and ग *ga* to ज *ja.*

57.—Other changes—many of them relating to single verbs—occur in the formation of this tense. At present the following examples may be committed to memory:—

भू	*bhú*	makes	बभूव	*babhúva*, he became.
गम्	*gam*	—	जगाम	*jagáma*, he went.
चर्	*char*	—	चचार	*chachára*, he went.
जि	*ji*	—	जिगाय	*jigáya*, he conquered.
तॄ	*tṛí*	—	ततार	*tatára*, he crossed over.
त्यज्	*tyaj*	—	तत्याज	*tatyája*, he abandoned.
दा	*dá*	—	ददौ	*dadau*, he gave.
दह्	*dah*	—	ददाह	*dadáha*, he burned.
दृश्	*dṛiś*	—	ददर्श	*dadarśa*, he saw.
द्रु	*dru*	—	दुद्राव	*dudráva*, it oozed.
पा	*pá*	—	पपौ	*papau*, he drank.
पच्	*pach*	—	पपाच	*papácha*, he cooked.
पत्	*pat*	—	पपात	*papáta*, he fell.
बुध्	*budh*	—	बुबोध	*bubodha*, he knew.
भ्रम्	*bhram*	—	बभ्राम	*babhráma*, he wandered.
वद्	*vad*	—	उवाद	*uváda*, he spoke.
वस्	*vas*	—	उवास	*uvása*, he dwelt.

वह	*vah*	makes	उवाह	*uváha*, he carried.
शुच्	*śuch*	—	शुशोच	*śuśocha*, he sorrowed for.
श्रि	*śri*	—	शिश्राय	*śiśráya*, he served.
श्रु	*śru*	—	शुश्राव	*śuśráva*, he heard.
सृ	*sṛi*	—	ससार	*sasára*, he went.
सृप्	*sṛip*	—	ससर्प	*sásarpa*, he crept.
स्मृ	*smṛi*	—	सस्मार	*sasmára*, he remembered.
स्रु	*sru*	—	सुस्राव	*susráva*, it dropped.
हस्	*has*	—	जहास	*jahása*, he laughed.
हृ	*hṛi*	—	जहार	*jahára*, he took.

Exercise 15.

58.—Translate the following phrases:—

रावणं जिगाय रामः। समुद्रं ततार कपिः। पुत्रस्त्याज पितरम्। अन्नं किमर्थं न पपाच नरः। पुष्पं कुतः पपात। ब्राह्मणः शास्त्रं बुबोध। नरः कुत्र बभ्राम। पिता पुत्रमुवाद। अश्वो नरमुवाह। जलं कुतः सुस्राव। नरो जलं पपौ। मृगो वनं चचार।

The horse fell. The man did not cross the ocean. The Bráhman remembered the scripture. The father, abandoned by the son, wandered. The jackal went to the shore. When did the boy laugh? He gave the food. The Bráhman heard the scripture. The girl served (her) mother. The fruit, taken by the hand, fell. The thief, seen by the man, crossed over the water. With anger, the enemy burnt the house.

Lesson 14.

59.—When an action succeeeus another—as when "Ráma conquered Rávaṉa, and went to his home"—the former action is commonly expressed by a participle called the *conjunctive*, which implies the *having done* so and so.

60.—The conjunctive participle (—in uncompounded verbs—) ends in त्वा *twá*. Ex. रामो रावणं जित्वा गृहं जगाम *rámo, rávaṉañ jitwá, grihañ jagáma*, 'Ráma, having conquered Rávaṉa went to his house (or home).'

61.—The following list of conjunctive participles may be committed to memory:

भूत्वा	*bhútwá*	having become.
त्यक्त्वा	*tyakwá*	having abandoned.
दत्त्वा	*dattwá*	having given.
हृत्वा	*hṛitwá*	having taken.
पीत्वा	*pítwá*	having drunk.
स्मृत्वा	*smṛitwá*	having remembered.
गत्वा	*gatwá*	having gone.
दृष्ट्वा	*dṛishṭwá*	having seen.
श्रुत्वा	*śrutwá*	having heard.
स्थित्वा	*sthitwá*	having stood.

Exercise 16.

62.—Translate the following phrases :—

The Bráhmaṉ, having gone to the shore, drinks water. The son, having abandoned the father, will wander. The men, having seen the tree, will go to the village. The jackal, having drunk water, went to the shore. The son, having remembered the father, spoke.

पुत्रः पित्रा त्यक्तो गृहं त्यक्त्वा भ्रमति । ब्राह्मणः शास्त्रं स्मृत्वा तीरं गत्वा जलं पपौ । मृगो नरं दृष्ट्वा चचार ।

नरः श्रुत्वा जहास । ब्राह्मणो जलं पीत्वा कुत्र गमिष्यति ।

Lesson 15.

63.—The following indeclinable words, including those given in Nos. 40 and 41, may be committed to memory.

VOCABULARY 4.

अकस्मात् *akasmât*, unexpectedly.

अत्र *atra*, here.

अद्य *adya*, to-day.

अन्यत्र *anyatra*, elsewhere.

इति *iti*, so, thus.

इव *iva*, like, as, so.

एकत्र *ekatra*, in one place.

एकधा *ekadhá*, in one way.

एवम् *evam*, thus, in this manner.

द्विधा *dwidhá*, in two ways.

कदा *kadá*, when?

किञ्च *kiñcha*, moreover.

किम् *kim*, what?

कुत्र *kutra*, where?

ततः *tatah*, thence, after that.

अतः *atah*, hence.

अथ *atha*, so, thus, well then.

अधुना *adhuná*, now.

अन्यथा *anyathá*, otherwise.

इदानीम् *idáním*, now.

इह *iha*, here.

एकदा *ekadá*, at one time, on one occasion.

एव *eva*, also, only.

कथम् *katham*, how? in what manner?

कदाचित् *kadáchit*, sometimes.

किन्तु *kintu*, but.

कुतः *kutah*, whence?

कुत्रचित् *kutrachit*, anywhere.

तत्र *tatra*, there.

तदा *tadá*, then.

तथाहि *tatháhi*, for thus, for example.

न *na*, not.

प्रायः *práyah*, mostly.

यदा *yadá*, when.

सर्वत्र *sarvatra*, everywhere.

तथा *tathá*, thus, so.

तावत *távat*, so far, so much. यथा *yathá*, as.

पश्चात् *paśchát*, afterwards. समीपे *samípe*, near to.

मध्ये *madhye*, in the midst of. सर्वदा *sarvadá*, always.

पुनर् *punar*, again. हि *hi*, verily, because.

64.—It may be observed, from the foregoing list, that the *interrogatives* begin with *k*, and the *relatives* with *y*. The termination of *time* is *dá*—as in तदा *tadá*, 'then;' that of *place* is *tra*—as in तत्र *tatra*, 'there.'

Lesson 16.

65.—The 4th, or *Dative*, case, and the 5th, or *Ablative*, case, of many words may be formed by the following substitutions.

		Sing.	Plural.
For final	Dat.	आय *áya*	एभ्यः *ebhyah.*
अ *a*	Abl.	आत् *át*	एभ्यः *ebhyah.*
For final	Dat.	अये *aye*	इभ्यः *ibhyah.*
इ *i*	Abl.	एः *eh*	इभ्यः *ibhyah*

Ex. रामाय *rámáya*, 'to Ráma;' रावणात् *rávaṉát*, 'from Rávaṉa;' नरेभ्यः *narebhyah*, 'to or from the men;' हरये *haraye*, 'to Hari;' कवेः *kaveh*, 'from the poet;' कविभ्यः *kavibhyah*, 'to or from the poets.'

Exercise 17.

66.—The father gave the book to the son. The girl goes from the house. Unexpectedly a flower fell from the tree. He gave wealth to the Bráhmaṉs. Rávaṉa, from anger, will not speak. He took water from the ocean. Then the king gave wealth to the poets. The arrow will fall again.

अकस्मात् पुनस्तीरात् पपात । पिता जलं दृष्ट्वा

पुत्राय हस्तं ददौ। ततो गत्वा ब्राह्मणाय धनं यच्छति। फलं वृक्षात् पतितं दृष्ट्वा पिता पुत्राय ददौ। कथं जलं हरति समुद्रात्। समीपे स्थित्वा समुद्रात् जलं जहार।

Lesson 17.

67.—The 6th, or *Genitive*, case, and the 7th, or *Locative*, case, of many words may be formed by the following substitutions.

		Singular.		Plural.	
For final अ *a*	Gen.	अस्य	*asya*	आनां	*ánám.*
	Loc.	ए	*e*	एषु	*eshu.*
For final इ *i*	Gen.	एः	*eh*	ईनां	*ínám.*
	Loc.	औ	*au*	इषु	*ishu.*

Ex रामस्य *rámasya*, 'of Ráma; समुद्रे *samudre*, 'in the ocean;' तीरे *tíre*, 'on the shore;' देवानां *devánám*, 'of the gods;' ग्रामेषु *grámeshu*, 'in the villages;' हरेः *hareh*, 'of Hari;' कवीनां *kavínám*, 'of the poets;' अग्नौ *agnau*, 'in the fire;' पतिषु *patishu*, 'among the masters.'

Exercise 18.

68.—Ráma dwells in the wood. He saw the house of Rávana. He sees a garland of flowers in the hand of the Bráhman. Men dwell in houses. The family of the jackal dwells in the wood. He stands in the midst of the fires. He saw the crow on the shore of the sea. He sees the flower fallen into the fire.

वृक्षे काको वसति। कन्या समुद्रस्य तीरे स्थित्वा चन्द्रं पश्यति। आरामं गत्वा वृक्षात् पतितं पुष्पं दृष्ट्वा मालिकः शुशोच। बालः कवीनां मध्ये स्थित्वा वदति। काकानां मध्ये बको न वसति। कवेर्वचनं श्रुत्वा राजा हसति।

Lesson 18.

69.—Adjectives, when declined, are declined like nouns. They are very commonly, however, prefixed, in their crude form, to the noun—and then they remain unaltered throughout the declension, forming a class of compounds termed *Karmmadháraya.* Thus the adjective कृष्ण *krishna*, 'black,' with the noun सर्प *sarpa*, 'a snake,' may be written कृष्णः सर्पः *krishnah sarpah*, or कृष्णसर्पः *krishnasarpa*, 'a black snake;' and again कृष्णेन सर्पेण *krishnena sarpena*, or कृष्णसर्पेण *krishnasarpena*, 'by a black snake.'

70.—The following list of adjectives may be committed to memory. An opposite meaning is given to an adjective by prefixing अ *a* or अन् *an*. Thus अतुल्य *atulya*, 'unlike;' अनुचित *anuchita*, 'improper.' In the neuter gender the adjectives may be used as adverbs. Thus शीघ्रं गच्छति *síghran gachchhati*, 'he goes quickly.'

VOCABULARY 5.

कृष्ण *krishna*, black.	संस्कृत *sanskrita*, polished.
शुक्ल *śukla*, white.	प्रिय *priya*, beloved.
नील *níla*, blue.	क्षुद्र *kshudra*, mean.
रक्त *rakta*, red.	अनन्त *ananta*, endless.
महत् *mahat*,* great.	चित्र *chitra*, variegated.
बहु *bahu*, much.	तुल्य *tulya*, like.
अल्प *alpa*, little.	दीर्घ *dírgha*, long.
शीघ्र *śíghra*, swift.	ह्रस्व *hraswa*, short.
मन्द *manda*, slow.	नव *nava*, new.
साधु *sádhu*, good.	व्याकुल *vyákulu*, perplexed.

* This usually becomes महा *mahá* in compound words.

शून्य *śúnya*, empty.

सुन्दर *sundara*, beautiful.

योग्य *yogya*, suitable.

वृद्ध *vṛiddha*, aged.

दक्षिण *dakshiṉa*, southern.

स्थूल *sthúla*, bulky.

दूर *dúra*, distant.

विस्मित *vismita*, astonished.

स्थिर *sthira*, firm.

पुराण *puráṉa*, old.

उचित *uchita*, proper.

Like the participles mentioned at No. 52, the adjectives that end in *a* generally make the feminine in *á* and the neuter in *am*. Thus प्रिया कन्या *priyá kanyá*, 'a beloved girl;' दक्षिणमरण्यं *dakshiṉam araṉyam*, 'the southern forest.'

Lesson 19.

71.—In the formation of *Karmmadháraya* (No. 69) and other compounds (as well as in cases where one word in a sentence immediately follows another—see No. 20—) some change often takes place in the two letters thus brought together. Some rules and remarks in regard to these changes here follow.

72.—*Similar* vowels are those that differ only in *length*. Thus *a* and *á* are similar; *i* and *í*; *u* and *ú*, &c. Others—as *i* and *u* —are *dissimilar*.

73.—Two *similar* vowels, meeting, coalesce and form one *long* vowel. Ex. *a* + *a* = *á*; *a* + *á* = *á*; *á* + *a* = *á*; *á* + *á* = *á*; *i* + *i* = *í*, &c.

74.—If a word end with *a* or *á* when the next begins with a *dissimilar* simple vowel, then a *guṉa* substitute (see No. 17) takes the place of the two concurring vowels. Thus *a* + *i* = *e*; *a* + *u* = *o*; *á* + *ṛi* = *ar*.

75.—If a word end with *a* or *á* when the next begins with a diphthong, then a substitute called *vṛiddhi* takes the place of the two concurring vowels. The *vṛiddhi* substitute of *e* or *ai* is *ai*; and that of *o* or *au* is *au*.

76.—If a word ends with *i*, *u*, or *ṛi*—short or long—when the next begins with any other dissimilar vowel, then *i* is changed to its semivowel *y*,—*u* to *v*, and *ri*, to *r*.

Exercise 19.

77.—Turn the following pairs of words into *Karmmadháraya* compounds—paying attention to the rules indicated as applicable to each—and putting each compound in the nominative singular.

संस्कृत *sañskṛita* + उक्ति *ukti* (No. 74), 'polished speech.' अनन्त *ananta* + आत्मन् *átman* (Nos. 73 and 74), 'the infinite soul.' नील *níla* + उत्पल *utpala*, 'a blue lotus.' महा *mahá* + ऋषि *ṛishi* (Nos. 74 and 17), 'a great sage.'

Lesson 20.

78.—When the case of a noun depends upon another noun or participle, the dependent noun may be prefixed in its crude form to the other, making the compound called *Tutpurusha.* For example 'the shore *of* the sea,' समुद्रस्य तीरं *samudrasya tíram,* may be expressed thus, समुद्रतीरं *samudra-tíram,* 'the sea-shore.'

79.—In a *Tutpurusha* compound the first term, in the crude form, has sometimes the force of a Genitive, sometimes of a Locative, &c. For example—in the compound पङ्कमग्न *pańka-magna* 'mud-sunk,' the word 'mud' has evidently the force of the Locative—the meaning being 'sunk in the mud.' Again—लोभाकृष्ट *lobhákṛishṭa,* 'greed-attracted,' evidently means 'attracted *by* greed'—the first term having the force of the Instrumental case.

Exercise 20.

80.—Turn the following pairs of words into *Tatpurusha* compounds—writing each compound in the Nominative singular.

'The influx (आगम *ágama*) of wealth (अर्थ *artha.*'—No. 73). 'A hundred (शत *śata* [n.]) of fools (मूर्ख *múrkha*).' 'Sport (क्रीडा *kríḍá*) in the water.' 'The shore of the Ganges (गङ्गा *gańgá*).' '[Who has] come (आगत *ágata*) for refuge

(शरण *śaraṇa*).' 'Deserted (हीन *hína*) by learning (विद्या *vidyá*).' 'Covered (वेष्टित *veshṭita*) with clothes (वस्त्र *vastra*).' 'A couple (द्वय *dwaya* [n.]) of verses (श्लोक *śloka*).' 'Lord (पति *pati*) of the earth (पृथिवी *prithví*).' 'The bank of a pond (सरस् *saras*).'

Exercise 21

ततः सरस्तीरं गत्वा ब्राह्मणो नीलोत्पलं ददर्श । एवं विद्याहीनं श्रुत्वा ब्राह्मणो दुःखेन व्याकुलो भविष्यति । लोभाकृष्टं पान्थं पङ्कमग्नं दृष्ट्वा हसति । ब्राह्मणस्य वचनं श्रुत्वा सभा विस्मिता बभूव ।

Lesson 21.

81.—The *Pronouns* are declined in most respects like nouns. The 1st and 2nd personal pronouns are very irregular. The following, being some of the most useful forms in which these present themselves, may be committed to memory.

Nom.	अहं *aham*, I.	वयं *vayam*, we.
Acc.	मां *mám*, me.	अस्मान् *asmán*, us.
Inst.	मया *mayá*, by me.	अस्माभिः *asmábhih*, by us.
Gen.	मम *mama*, my.	अस्माकं *asmákam*, our.

Nom.	त्वं *twam*, thou.	यूयं *yúyam*, you.
Acc.	त्वां *twám*, thee.	युष्मान् *yushmán*, you.
Inst.	त्वया *twayá*, by thee.	युष्माभिः *yushmábhih*, by you.
Gen.	तव *tava*, thy.	युष्माकं *yushmákam*, your.

	Singular	Plural
Nom.	सः *sah*, he (or 'that').	ते *te*, they (or 'those').
Acc.	तं *tam*, him.	तान् *tán*, them.
Inst.	तेन *tena*, by him.	तैः *taih*, by them.
Dat.	तस्मै *tasmai*, to him.	तेभ्यः *tebhyah*, to them.
Abl.	तस्मात् *tasmát*, from him.	तेभ्यः *tebhyah*, from them.
Gen.	तस्य *tasya*, his.	तेषां *teshám*, of them.
Loc.	तस्मिन *tasmin*, in him.	तेषु *teshu*, in them.

82.—The feminine of this pronoun is सा *sá*, 'she,' or 'that' In the neuter we have तद् *tad*, 'that,' and तानि *táni*, 'those.'

83.—A useful demonstrative pronoun is formed by prefixing ए *e* to the foregoing. Thus एषः *eshah*, 'he,' 'this;' एतद् *etad*, 'this.' The pronoun इदं *idam*, 'this,' makes अयं *ayam* in the Nominative singular masculine.

84.—As observed at No. 64, the *interrogatives begin* with *k*, and the *relatives* with *y*. Thus कः *kah*, 'who?' कस्मात् *kasmát*, 'from whom?' or, 'from what?' यः *yah*, 'who,' यस्मात् *yasmát*, 'from whom,' or, 'from which.'

85.—The Nom. sing. neut. of कः *kah* is किं *kim*, 'what?'

86.—The indeclinable affixes *chit*, *api*, and *chana*, added to the several cases of the *interrogative* pronoun, give them an indefinite signification. Thus कश्चित् *kaśchit*, (No. 25) 'somebody,' or, 'anybody;'—केनचित् *kenachit*, 'by some one;'—किञ्चित् *kinchit* 'something.'

Exercise 22.

87.—Write the following phrases in Sanskrit.

Where is my son? Where is thy book? The jackal, seen by thee, will abandon the forest. The crow, seen by me, abandons the tree. When (was) this speech heard by him? By whom (was) the speech of the Bráhmaṉ heard? Where does their father dwell? This is our house. Where is your house? Who sees you? Some one sees you. Who dwell in those houses? This speech (was) heard by a certain Bráhmaṉ. The king gave wealth to him.

Lesson 22.

88.—The mas. nom. sing. सः *sah,* 'he,' 'that,' and एषः *eshah* 'this,' drop the *visarga* when a consonant follows. Thus स गच्छति *sa gachchhati,* 'he goes;' एष मनुष्यः *esha manushyah* 'this man.'

89.—The conjunction '*and*' is expressed by च *cha,* which is placed after the second word. Thus पिता पुत्रश्च *pitá putraścha,* 'the father and the son.' In the same way the conjunction वा *vá,* 'or':—thus पिता पुत्रोवा *pitá putra vá,* 'the father or the son.'

Vocabulary 6.

किन्तु *kintu,* but.	अपि *api,* also, even.
यदि *yadi,* if.	चेत् *chet,* if.
तर्हि *tarhi,* then, in that case.	नो चेत् *no chet,* if not.
परन्तु *parantu,* but, on the other hand.	हि *hi,* because.

90.—When the subject or object of the verb is a whole clause, the clause is concluded by the conjunction इति *iti,* 'thus.' For example:—रावणो रामेण जित इति मया श्रुतं *rávano rámeṉa jita, iti mayá śrutam,* 'Rávaṉa was conquered by Ráma—thus (has been) heard by me:'— or रावणो रामेण जित इति वदति वाल्मीकिः *rávaṉo rámeṉa jita, iti vadati válmíkih,* 'Válmíki says Rávaṉa was conquered by Ráma.'

Exercise 23.

A tiger also dwells in the southern forest. Then he dwelt in a garden, but now he wanders on the sea-shore. Something fell again. In our village is a master of poets. When is an empty house beautiful? The girl and her aged father and mother are here. The poet says the tiger went to Káśí. Is this man or that boy suitable? Unexpectedly a mouse fell from the seat. Again the Bráhmaṇs cross over the water. Everywhere he conquered the enemy. Thus the monkey will burn their houses. The horse went, but the jackal even now stands. Sometimes the devotee wandered here. The traveller heard the sound of a lute somewhere. That man knew the scriptures. After that he went slowly to the old tree. Thus he took the books and the arrows, with (his) hand, from the thief. Among the Bráhmaṇs is a good preceptor. He will sometimes cook the food suitably. The preceptor says, Who laughed then?

Lesson 23.

91.—In making the *passive voice* of the present and some of the other tenses, the letter य *ya* is added to the root—and the terminations called the *átmane-pada* are subjoined. Thus, the *átmane-pada* termination of the 3d pers. sing. present being ते *te*, we have दह्यते *dahyate*, 'it is burned,' पच्यते *pachyate*, 'it is cooked,' &c.

92.—Some verbs are conjugated in the active voice, with the terminations called the *átmane-pada*. For example:

यत्	*yat*, 'to strive'	makes	यतते	*yatate*,	'he strives.'
रम्	*ram*, 'to sport'	—	रमते	*ramate*,	'he sports.'
लोच	*loch*, 'to see'	—	लोचते	*lochate*,	'he sees.'
वृत्	*vrit*, 'to be'	—	वर्त्तते	*varttate*,	'he is.'
शुभ्	*śubh*, 'to shine'	—	शोभते	*śobhate*,	'he shines.'
षह्	*shah*, 'to endure'	—	सहते	*sahate*,	'he endures.'
षेव्	*shev*, 'to serve'	—	सेवते	*sevate*,	'he serves.'
ष्मि	*shmi*, 'to smile'	—	स्मयते	*smayate*,	'he smiles.'

Exercise 24.

Translate the following sentences.

The crow is seen by the jackal. The father is abandoned by the son. The oblation is burned by the fire. The food is cooked by the man. The deer sports in the forest. The Bráhman endures pain. The girl smiles. He sees crows on the tree. The king shines in the assembly. Why is the gardener perplexed?

पिता पुत्रेण त्यक्तो दुःखं सहते । राजा कवेर्वचनं श्रुत्वा स्मयते । तव पुस्तकं कुत्र वर्त्तते । कन्या सरस्तीरे स्थित्वा नीलोत्पलं लोचते । पुत्रेण सरस्तीरे स्थित्वा नीलोत्पलं लोच्यते ॥

Lesson 24.

93.—Verbs of the 2nd conjugation do not insert the vowel *a* before the tense-affixes (No. 17). Thus the verb अस् *us*, 'to be,' makes अस्ति *asti*, 'he is.'

Of the verb 'to be' the following portions may be committed to memory.

Present.

Singular.	*Plural.*
अस्ति *asti*, he is.	सन्ति *santi*, they are.

1st Preterite.

आसीत् *ásít*, he was.	आसन् *ásan*, they were.

Imperative.

अस्तु *astu*, let it be.	सन्तु *santu*, let them be.

Potential.

स्यात् *syát*, 'he may (or should) be.' स्युः *syuh*, 'they may be.'

Exercise 25.

There is in that wood a certain tree. Thy father is not in the house. There was water everywhere. Thus let it be, said the Bráhmaṉ. The son should not be perplexed. In the empty village was an aged jackal. Let the horses be beautiful. The garden is distant. The preceptors should be good men. He says it is proper. That man said it was improper. Having seen the deer sunk in the mud, the jackal laughed.

कुत्र सन्ति मम पुस्तकानि । आसीत् तस्मिन् वने कश्चन शृगालः । यदि तथा स्यात् तर्हि पिता व्याकुलो भविष्यति । तस्य वचनं श्रुत्वा कथं व्याकुलाः स्युः ।

94.—In addition to the rules for the treatment of *visarga* given in Nos. 21, 24, and 48, it is to be observed that अः *ah*, when any vowel but short अ *a* follows, drops the *visarga*. Thus शृगाल आसीत् *ṣrigála ásít*, 'there was a jackal.'

95.—The vowel अ *a* drops when it comes after a word ending in ओ *o* or ए *e*. Thus नरो ऽद्य *naro' dya*, 'the man today;' ते ऽत्र न सन्ति *te 'tra na santi* 'they are not here.' The character ऽ serves, like an apostrophe, to mark the place of the expunged vowel.

Lesson 25.

The following are useful verbs of the 2nd conjugation.

ब्रू	*brú*, to speak (or say).	ब्रूते	*brúte*, he speaks.
वच्	*vach*, to speak.	वक्ति	*vakti*, he speaks.
या	*yá*, to go.	याति	*yáti*, he goes.
ष्णा	*shṉá*, to bathe.	स्नाति	*snáti*, he bathes.
हन्	*han*, to kill.	हन्ति	*hanti*, he kills.

96.—The characteristic peculiarity of the 3d conjugation is the reduplication of the radical syllable. For examples:—दा *dá*, 'to give' makes ददाति *dadáti*, 'he gives.'

97.—The characteristic of the 4th conjugation is य *ya*. Examples:—

क्षिप् *kship*, to throw. क्षिप्यति *kshipyati*, he throws.

जन् *jan*, to be produced. जायते *jáyate*, it is produced.

णश् *ṉaś*, to perish. नश्यति *naśyati*, he perishes.

पद् *pad*, to go. पद्यते *padyate*, he goes.

युध् *yudh*, to fight. युध्यते *yudhyate*, he fights.

विद् *vid*, to exist. विद्यते *vidyate*, it exists.

98.—The characteristic of the 5th conjugation is the syllable नु *nu*—changeable, under ordinary circumstances, to नो *no*. Examples:—

आप् *áp*, to obtain. आप्नोति *ápnoti*, he obtains.

शक् *śak*, to be able. शक्नोति *śaknoti*, he is able.

99.—The 6th conjugation, like the 1st, takes a short अ *a* but does not, like the 1st, substitute *guṉa* (No. 17). Examples:—

तृप् *tṛip*, to satisfy. तृपति *tṛipati*, he satisfies.

इष् *ish*, to wish इच्छति *ichchhati*, he wishes.

प्रच्छ् *prachchh*, to ask. पृच्छति *pṛichchhati*, he asks.

मृ *mṛi*, to die. म्रियते *mriyate*, he dies.

स्पृश् *spṛiś*, to touch. स्पृशति *spṛiśati*, he touches.

100.—The 7th conjugation, in certain tenses, inserts न *na* before the final of the root. Examples:—

भिद् *bhid*, to break. भिनत्ति *bhinatti*, he breaks.

हिस् *his*, to injure. हिनस्ति *hinasti*, he injures.

101.—The 8th conjugation adds उ *u* (which in certain cases becomes ओ *o*). Examples:—

कृ *kṛi*, to do or make. करोति *karoti*, he makes.

Other parts of this verb are चकार *chakára*, 'he made;' करिष्यति *karishyati*, 'he will make;' कुर्य्यात् *kuryyát*, 'he should make.'

102.—The 9th conjugation subjoins ना *ná*. Examples:—

ग्रह् *grah*, to take. गृह्णाति *gṛihṇáti*, he takes.

ज्ञा *jná*, to know. जानाति *jánáti*, he knows.

103.—The 10th conjugation subjoins इ *i*, which is liable, among other things, to be changed to its improper diphthong ए *e*, and that again, before a vowel, to अय *ay* (by No. 18). Examples:—

कथ् *kath*, to tell. कथयति *kathayati*, he tells.

चित् *chit*, to think. चिन्तयति *chintayati*, he thinks.

मन्त्र् *matr*, to advise. मन्त्रयति *mantrayati*, he advises.

Exercise 26.

Translate the following sentences.

The son says. Ráma kills Rávaṇa. The king gives wealth to the Bráhmaṇ. The girl throws the flowers. How is a blue lotus produced here? Rávaṇa fights, but, conquered by Ráma, he perishes. An enemy of that man does not exist anywhere. He obtains wealth. Not any one is able. He satisfies the sons with food. What does that man wish? Why does not any one ask him? The man, having gone to the sea-shore, dies. The girl does not touch the flower. The son breaks the fruit from the tree. The good man does not injure any one. What is he doing? He takes the book. No one knows. Why does he not tell? Thus he thinks. He does not thus advise.

Lesson 26.

In the following exercise the verbs given in the preceding lesson are exhibited in the various forms treated of in Nos. 28, 30, 39, 52, 55, 57, and 61,—a reference to which rules may enable the learner to translate the phrases.

Exercise 27.

कुत्र जायन्ते नीलोत्पलानि । फलं क्षिप्त्वा गच्छति । कथं न कथयिष्यति । एवं चिन्तयित्वा वदति । एवं ज्ञात्वा समुद्रतीरं गच्छति । कदाचित् तथा न कुर्य्यात् । पिता पुत्रं गृहीत्वा गृहं गच्छति । शुक्लाः काका न विद्यन्ते कुत्रचित् । को ऽस्त्ययं नरः । उत्पलानि तत्र जातानि नीलानि न सन्ति परन्तु शुक्लानि। फलं गृहीत्वा ग्रामं गच्छति । कुत्र याति । कदा स्नास्यति ।

If the disciple shall ask, then he will obtain; if not, he will not obtain. Having seen the ocean, he goes to the mountain. The monkey sports in the garden, and in the wood, and on the bank of the pond. They say the traveller will die. Why do the boys break the garlands? Sometimes he speaks improperly. The beautiful girl bathes in the ocean. Having drunk water he goes to the sacrifice. Thus he wandered and there he dwelt. The father, having seen (his) son, smiles. Everywhere and always disciples thus serve (their) preceptors. They endure great pain. The Bráhman, deserted by learning, does not shine in the assembly. Sin is produced by anger. Good men quickly obtain great prosperity.

Lesson 27.

104.—Two or more words coupled together by the conjunction '*and*' may, with omission of the 'and,' be made into a compound called a *Dwandwa*. If there be only two words in it, the compound takes the terminations of the *Dual* number. The *nom. dual* termination of a noun ending in अ *a* is औ *au*. Thus 'Ráma and Lakshmaṇa' may be expressed by either रामो लक्ष्मणश्च *rámo-lakshmaṇascha*, or रामलक्ष्मणौ *ráma-lakshmaṇau*.

105.—When a *Dwandwa* compound contains more than two terms, it generally takes the termination of the plural. Example:—ब्राह्मणक्षत्रियविट्शूद्राः *bráhmaṇa-kshatriya-viṭ-śúdráh*, 'the Bráhmaṇ, and Kshatriya, and Vaiśya, and Śúdra.'

106.—Verbs, as well as nouns and pronouns, have a dual number. The 3d pers. dual of the present tense ends in तः *tah*. Thus रामलक्ष्मणौ वने वसतः *ráma-lakshmaṇau vane vasatah*; 'Ráma and Lakshmaṇa dwell in the forest:—काकौ वृक्षे वसतः *kákau vṛikshe vasatah*, 'two crows dwell in the tree.'

107.—When two or more words are put together to form an *epithet*, the compound is called a *Bahuvríhi*. For example:—नामधेय *námadheya*, meaning a 'name,' we may have the epithet पाटलिपुत्रनामधेय *pâṭaliputra-námadheya*, 'the name of which is Páṭaliputra.' Such an epithet, like an adjective, agrees with its noun. Thus पाटलिपुत्रनामधेयं नगरं *páṭaliputra-námadheyan nagaram*, 'a city named Páṭaliputra:'—कुशहस्तो नरः *kuśa-hasto narah*, 'a man with kuśa-grass in his hand.'

108.—A word in the genitive case very commonly dispenses with the case-ending, and forms a *Tatpurusha* compound with the governing word. Thus देवानां याजकः *devánám yájakah*, 'a worshipper of the gods,' may be expressed by देवयाजकः *deva-yájakah*. In the majority of instances the *Tatpurusha* compound involves a genitive case, but words in other cases can enter into composition in this way. For example, we have the instrumental case in काकपेय *káka-peya*, 'to be drunk by a crow,'—applied to a river with muddy water, fit only for a crow's beverage.

109.—The changes (referred to in No. 71) when heterogeneous letters come together, in compounds or in sentences, are not confined to the vowels. The principal rule in regard to the changes of the consonants is the following.

110.—A hard consonant (No. 24) before a soft consonant is changed to the soft of its own class; and *vice versâ*. Thus महत् *mahat* + भय *bhaya* = महद्भय *mahadbhaya*, 'great fear.'

111.—A dental consonant coming before a palatal or a cerebral is changed to a corresponding letter:—for example तत् च *tat cha* becomes तच्च *tachcha*, 'and that.' The pronunciation is not so much altered by this, but that one who knows the separate words can readily recognise them when so combined. The same remark applies to the change of न *na* to ण *ṉa* in certain cases —as when preceded by र् *ra*.

112.—The letters त् *t* and श् *ś* meeting become च्छ् *chchh*. The commonest instance of this occurs in तत् *tat* + श्रुत्वा *śrutwá* = तच्छ्रुत्वा *tachchhrutwá*, 'having heard that.'

Exercise 28.

The two sons go to the sea-shore. The crow and the jackal dwell in the forest. Having heard that, the deer abandons the forest. There is, on the bank of the Ganges, a city named Káśí. Why do the preceptor and the disciple again go to the garden? When will the snake, the mouse, and the horse dwell in one place? Men of slow understanding are infinite. A man of great wealth wishes thus. A boy and a girl of good family are here. A village of empty houses is not distant. A man of great merit says so. A boy beloved by (his) mother and a girl beloved by (her) father are here.

Lesson 28.

113.—In the native Sanskrit grammar, all the varieties of declension are educed from a set of technical terminations which the learner will find it well worth his while to commit to memory. They are to be read across the page—thus "*su, au, jas,*" &c.

	Sing.		Dual.		Plur.	
Nom.	सु	*su.*	औ	*au.*	जस्	*jas.*
Acc.	अं	*am.*	औट्	*auṭ.*	शस्	*śas.*
Inst.	टा	*ṭá.*	भ्यां	*bhyám.*	भिस्	*bhis.*
Dat.	ङे	*ńe.*	भ्यां	*bhyám.*	भ्यस्	*bhyas.*
Abl.	ङसि	*ńasi.*	भ्यां	*bhyám.*	भ्यस्	*bhyas.*
Gen.	ङस्	*ńas.*	ओस्	*os.*	आं	*ám.*
Loc.	ङि	*ńi.*	ओस्	*os.*	सुप्	*sup.*

114.—The vocative has no separate termination, it being considered as a modification only of the nominative.

115.—Now, of these inflectional terminations it is to be remarked, that some of the letters serve only to form syllables and to facilitate enunciation: they disappear, therefore, when those letters which are essential are applied to the word to be declined. These auxiliary letters are the *u* of *su*; the *j* of *jas*; the *ś* of *śas*; the *ṭ* of *auṭ* and *ṭá*; the *ń* everywhere; the *i* of *ńasi*; and the *p* of *sup*. It is also to be observed that a final स् *s* is changed to *visarga*. The actual terminations therefore will be :—

	Sing.		Dual.		Plur.	
Nom.	:	*h*	औ	*au.*	अः	*ah.*
Acc.	अं	*am.*	औ	*au.*	अः	*ah.*
Inst.	आ	*á.*	भ्यां	*bhyám.*	भिः	*bhih.*
Dat.	ए	*e.*	भ्यां	*bhyám.*	भ्यः	*bhyah.*
Abl.	अः	*ah.*	भ्यां	*bhyám.*	भ्यः	*bhyah.*
Gen.	अः	*ah.*	ओः	*oh.*	आं	*ám.*
Loc.	इ	*i.*	ओः	*oh.*	सु	*su.*

116.—In applying these terminations to the final letter of the word to be declined, recollection must be had of the rules for the permutation of vowels and consonants. For example, in declining the word नौ *nau*, 'a ship,' it must be remembered that औ *au*, followed by a vowel, becomes आव् *áv;* and that स् *s* becomes ष् *sh* when it follows any other vowel than *a* or *á* and is not final. Thus :—

	Sing.	*Dual.*	*Plur.*
Nom.	नौः *nauh,* a ship.	नावौ *návau,* two ships.	नावः *návah,* [ships.
Acc.	नावं *návam,* a ship,	नावौ *návau,*	नावः *navah,*
Inst.	नावा *ná vá,* by —	नौभ्यां *naubhyám,*	नौभिः *naubhih,*
Dat.	नावे *náve,* to —	नौभ्यां *naubhyám,*	नौभ्यः *naubhyah,*
Abl.	नावः *návah,* from	नौभ्यां *naubhyám,*	नौभ्यः *náubhyah,*
Gen.	नावः *návah,* of —	नावोः *návoh,*	नावां *návám,*
Loc.	नावि *návi,* in —	नावोः *návoh,*	नौषु *naushu,*

Exercise 29.

Write down, with the signification, the following cases of the following words, viz.:—

Inst. sing., inst. plu., and loc. plu., of उक्ति *ukti,* 'speech.' Gen. sing. and inst. sing. of आत्मन् *átman,* 'soul' or 'self.' Loc. sing. and gen. plu. of दिश् *diś,* 'a side' or 'direction.' Loc. sing, of मनस् *manas,* 'the mind.' Inst. sing. and inst. plu. of अग्नि *agni,* 'fire.' Nom. dual and loc. plu. of नदी *nadí,* 'a river.' Loc. plu. of स्त्री *strí,* 'a woman.' Dat. sing., inst. plu., and loc. plu. of पितृ *pitṛi,* 'a father.' Inst. sing., dat. sing., abl. sing., inst. plu., and gen. plu. of वाच् *vách,* 'speech.' Inst. sing. of मरुत् *marut*, 'the wind.' Loc. sing. of शरद् *śarad*, 'autumn.' Gen. plu. of धीमत् *dhímat*, 'sensible.' Loc. sing. of सरस् *saras*, 'a pond.' Gen. plu. of मधुलिह् *madhu-lih*, 'a bee.'

Lesson 29.

117.—As the native Sanskrit grammar presents one scheme of terminations which, by means of the requisite substitutions, may be accommodated to all nouns, so it presents one scheme of terminations which, with the requisite substitutions, becomes applicable to all the tenses of every verb. These terminations are enunciated in a different order, as regards *person*, from that to which the European reader is accustomed,—the personality applicable to what is spoken of being the first, and that applicable to the speaker being the third. Instead of naming the persons by *numbers*, therefore, it may be advisable here to give them the epithets appropriated to them in the native grammar,—calling that which *is spoken of* the 'Lowest,' the one *spoken to* the 'Middle,' and the *speaker* the 'Highest' person.

118.—The terminations are as follows:—

	Sing.	*Dual.*	*Plur.*
Lowest.	तिप् *tip.*	तस् *tas.*	झि *jhi.*
Middle.	सिप् *sip.*	थस् *thas.*	थ *tha.*
Highest.	मिप् *mip.*	वस् *vas.*	मस् *mas.*

119.—In these, as in the inflectional terminations of nouns, (No. 113), some of the letters serve to indicate certain operations; and these are rejected when the termination is affixed to the verb. After the requisite rejections and substitutions, the terminations appear as follows:—

ति *ti.*	तः *tah.*	अन्ति *anti.*
सि *si.*	थः *thah.*	थ *tha.*
मि *mi.*	वः *vah.*	मः *mah.*

120.—Adding these terminations to the root अद् *ad*, 'to eat,' and changing its final soft consonant to a hard one (No. 110) when the affix begins with a hard consonant, we have

अत्ति *atti*, he eats.	अत्तः *attah*, they two eat.	अदन्ति [*adanti*, they eat.
अत्सि *atsi* thou eatest.	अत्थः *atthah*, you two eat.	अत्थ [*attha*, you eat.
अद्मि *admi*, I eat.	अद्वः *adwah*, we two eat.	अद्मः [*admah*, we eat.

121.—When the short vowel *a* precedes the *m* or *v* of the tense-affix, it is lengthened. Thus we have भवामि *bhavámi*, 'I become:'—भविष्यामि *bhavishyámi*, 'I will become.'

122.—In order that the foregoing set of terminations may serve for other tenses than the present, they require to be variously modified. For instance, as may be gathered from No. 28, the syllable स्य *sya* requires to be interposed when the sense is to be future. Again, to express time past, (that of the 1st preterite) the final *i* of the singular is dropped, and the vowel अ *a* is prefixed to the verb as an augment. Thus अभवत् *abhavat*, 'he became.'

123.—अहं 'I,' त्वं 'thou,' and सः 'he,' are declined in the dual as follows:—

Nom.	आवां	युवां	तौ
Acc.	———	———	———
Inst.	आवाभ्यां	युवाभ्यां	ताभ्यां
Dat.	———	———	———
Abl.	———	———	———
Gen.	आवयोः	युवयोः	तयोः
Loc.	———	———	———

Exercise 30.

Translate the following sentences.

Who art thou? I go to the village. They two will go to the village. Do you two go to the wood? Shall we two go to the sea-shore? Thou seest my house. What dost thou? What dost thou wish? What dost thou say? I do not say anything. Art thou able, or not? I am not able. I see thy son.

अद्य वयं क्व गच्छामः । यूयं समुद्रे न स्नाथ । तौ कस्मात् युध्यतः । भवान् कविर्न वा । अहमित्थं चिन्तयामि । अहं ग्रामं पुनर्गमिष्यामि । बालकौ सरसि नष्टौ । अहमित्थं करिष्यामीति त्वं कुतो न वदसि ।

Lesson 30.

124.—The *infinitive* is formed by adding तुं *tum*. Ex. यातुं *yátum*, 'to go.'

Many verbs insert इ *i* before तुं. Ex. भवितुं *bhavitum*, 'to become.'

The following is a list of infinitives.

कृ	*kṛi*	makes	कर्त्तुं	*karttum*, to make.
गम्	*gam*	—	गन्तुं	*gantum*, to go.
जि	*ji*	—	जेतुं	*jetum*, to conquer.
दा	*dá*	—	दातुं	*dátum*, to give.
दृश्	*dṛiś*	—	द्रष्टुं	*drashṭum*, to see.
ष्ठा	*shṭhá*	—	स्थातुं	*sthátum*, to stay.
वच्	*vach*	—	वक्तुं	*vaktum*, to speak.

Exercise 31.

Translate the following sentences.

Rávaṉa is not able to conquer Ráma. The father wishes to give the book to the son. The two sons wish to go to the wood. Dost thou wish to go to the sea-shore? I wish to see my father. Do you two wish to stay here? What dost thou wish to do? It is improper to do thus. To speak thus is unsuitable.

भक्ताः पर्वतं गन्तुमिच्छन्ति । त्वं अरुन्धतीं तारां द्रष्टुं न शक्नोषि । नावस्तीरं यातुं न शक्ताः । अत्र स्यातुमुचितम् । तत्र स्यातुं योग्यमिति पिता ब्रवीति । मन्दं वक्तुमुचितमस्ति । वृद्धेभ्यो धनं दातुं योग्यं ।

Lesson 31.

125.—The *present participle active* ends in अत् *at.* Thus भवत् *bhavat,* 'being;' गच्छत् *gachchhat,* 'going;' तिष्ठत् *tishṭhat,* 'staying.'

This participle is declined as follows:—

Sing. { Nom. गच्छन् *gachchhan,* 'going.'
Acc. गच्छन्तं *gachchhantam.*

Dual Nom. and Acc. गच्छन्तौ *gachchhantau.*

Plu. Nom. गच्छन्तः *gachchhantah.*

The rest of the declension may be effected by subjoining the terminations from No. 114.

126.—The *indefinite past participle active* ends in तवत् *tavat:*—as कृतवत् *kṛitavat,* 'was making.' It is declined like the present participle (No. 125), except that it takes a long vowel in the nom. sing.,—thus कृतवान् *kṛitaván.* It is commonly used with an auxiliary verb—thus अहं कृतवानस्मि *ahań kṛitaván asmi,* 'I was doing.'

127.—A class of *future participles*, most extensively employed, is formed by the affixes तव्य *tavya*, अनीय *aníya*, and य *ya*. Examples. भवितव्य *bhavitavya*, 'what is to be or ought to be;' सहनीय *sahaníya*, 'what is to be endured;' लभ्य *labhya*, 'to be acquired.'

The following are further examples :—

वक्तव्य	*vaktavya*,	to be spoken.
भज्य	*bhajya*,	to be worshipped.
शक्य	*śakya*,	possible.
सह्य	*sahya*,	endurable.
कार्य्य	*káryya*,	to be made, or done.
द्रष्टव्य	*drashṭavya*,	to be seen.
गन्तव्य	*gantavya*,	to be gone.

128.—The future participle is much used in the nom. sing. neuter. Thus त्वया गन्तव्यं *twayá gantavyam*, 'it is to be gone by thee'—*i. e.* 'thou art to go:'—तथा भवितव्यं तेन 'thus is it to be become by him'—*i. e.* 'thus must he become.'

Exercise 32.

Translate the following sentences.

तथा कदापि न मया कर्त्तव्यम् । अहं दक्षिणारण्ये गच्छन् वृद्धव्याघ्रमपश्यम् । स व्याघ्रः सरसि स्नात्वा कुशहस्तो वदति । हे पान्थ कुत्र त्वया गन्तव्यं । दुःखं सहनीयमस्ति रावणेन । किं कर्त्तव्यं मम पुत्रैः ।

Lesson 32.

129.—Verbs compounded with prepositions sometimes retain the meaning of the original; more frequently they have the sense of their component elements; but in many instances they have significations which depart widely from those which they might be expected, from their composition, to convey. The explanation of such compounds is the province of the dictionary.

130.—Of the twenty-one prepositions, the most useful here follow, the sense being exemplified in verbs or in derivatives, of frequent occurrence, from verbs compounded with the prepositions.

अति *ati*, 'beyond.' अतिक्रामति *atikrámati*, 'he goes beyond.'

अधि *adhi*, 'over.' अधिगत *adhigata*, 'gone over' (as a book when read through).

अनु *anu*, 'after, like.' अनुचरति *anucharati*, 'he goes after' (as a disciple goes after and imitates his preceptor).

अप *apa*, 'off.' अपहरति *apaharati*, 'he carries off.'

अभि *abhi*, 'opposite.' अभिगच्छति *abhigachchhati*, 'he approaches.'

आ *á*, 'reversing.' आगच्छति *ágachchhati*, 'he comes.'

आददाति *ádadáti*, 'he takes.'

उप *upa*, 'near.' उपतिष्ठते *upatishṭhate*, 'he stands near.'

निर् *nir*, 'without.' निर्दोष *nirdosha*, 'without fault.'

परि *pari*, 'around.' परिधि *paridhi*, 'perimeter.'

प्रति *prati*, 'again, back.' प्रतीकार *pratíkára*, 'retaliation.'

प्रतिदिनं *pratidinam*, 'day by day.'

वि *vi*, 'apart.' वियोग *viyoga*, 'disjunction.'

विकार *vikára*, 'change of form.'

सं *sam*, 'with.' सङ्गम *sangama*, 'association.'

131.—Of prepositions used separately or without verbs, प्रति *prati*, 'towards,' governs the accusative; सह *saha*, 'with,' governs the instrumental, and विना *viná*, 'without, except,' either the accusative or the instrumental.

Exercise 33.

Translate the following sentences.

This book is to be gone over by thee. The disciples go after the preceptor. Rávaṇa carries off Sítá. The traveller approaches the tiger. The traveller does not approach the tiger without fear. The father, with the son, stands near the tree. The crow does not associate with the jackal. Day by day the crow and the jackal associate with the deer. How is their disjunction to be made?

धर्ममतिक्रामति प्रतिदिनम् । शिष्या अनुचरिष्यन्ति गुरुम् । सीतामपजहार रावणः । भयं विना व्याघ्रो नोपगन्तव्यः । पुत्रः पितरमुपतिष्ठते । अत्र प्रतीकारो न कर्त्तव्यः । कुत आगतो ऽयं शृगालः । पुत्रस्य हस्तात् पिता पुस्तकमाददाति । अनधिगतशास्त्रा मम पुत्राः किं वक्तुं शक्नुवन्ति ।

Lesson 33.

132.—It will have been observed, in Lesson 24, that the 3d pers. sing. of the imperative ends in तु. In the *passive* the termination is तां *tám*—preceded by the य *ya* of the passive (No. 91). Thus श्रूयतां *śrúyatám*, 'let it be heard;' क्रियतां *kriyatám*, 'let it be done;' दृश्यतां *dṛiśyatám*, 'let it be seen;' उच्यतां *uchyatám*, 'let it be told.'

133.—In Lesson 24, the *potential* is exhibited ending in यात् *yát*—as कुर्य्यात् *kuryyát*, 'he should make:'—but the form in which it is more commonly met with is that of the 1st conjugation, where it ends in एत् *et.* Thus भवेत् *bhavet,* 'he should be;' भवेयुः *bhaveyuh,* 'they should be.'

Exercise 34.

Translate the following sentences:—

The preceptor should be a good man. The horse should be white. The disciple should not be perplexed. Let the wish be heard by the father. Let the deer sport in the forest. Let the beautiful girl smile. Let the crow go. Why should it be improper to do thus? He should obtain merit. They should go home. Let not injury be done to any one.

वने पान्थो न नश्येत् । माता ऽन्यथा जानीयात् । प्रभुर्म्मन्त्रयेत् । शिष्यः कवेः पुस्तकानि गृह्णीयात् । वको जले स्नायात् । वृद्धं व्याघ्रं न हिंस्यात् । पितुर्गृहे पूजां कुर्य्यात् । अस्य पुस्तकस्य द्वितीयभागः पश्चात् प्रकाशितो भवेत् ।

PART II.

BEING AN INTRODUCTION TO THE HITOPADESÁ.

Professor Johnson, in the Preface to his very useful edition of the *Hitopadeśa*, "with a grammatical analysis alphabetically arranged," notices, among the other recommendations of that interesting collection of Sanskrit tales, that "In no single work is there to be met with a more comprehensive assemblage of serviceable words and phrases." "The moral verses with which the *Hitopadeśa* abounds are (Mr. Johnson tells us), in many cases, perhaps in all, quotations from different writers. They consequently form a sort of anthology,—a collection of passages, not only remarkable for striking thoughts, but offering examples of various styles." These verses being considerably more difficult of construction than the stories in which they are inserted, the beginner will run the less risk of being disheartened if he be required to construe the stories only in the first place, —the verses (—except where they may be indispensable to the narrative, or otherwise deserving of immediate notice—) being laid aside for future consideration.

After some introductory verses, the compiler of the *Hitopadeśa* proceeds as follows:—

Extract 1.

अस्ति भागीरथीतीरे पाटलिपुत्रनामधेयं नगरम्। तत्र सर्वस्वामिगुणोपेतः सुदर्शनो नाम नरपतिरासीत्।

The king here mentioned having a set of idle sons, he secured the services of the learned *Vishṇuśarman*, who undertook to reclaim them by telling them stories calculated to excite in them an interest in political affairs. The narrative proceeds as follows:—

अथ प्रासादपृष्ठे सुखोपविष्टानां राजपुत्राणां पुरस्तात् प्रस्तावक्रमेण स पण्डितोऽब्रवीत् । भो राजपुत्राः शृणुत ।

काव्यशास्त्रविनोदेन कालो गच्छति धीमताम् ।
व्यसनेनच मूर्खाणां निद्रया कलहेन वा ॥

तद्भवतां विनोदाय काककूर्मादीनां विचित्रां कथां कथयामि । राजपुत्रैरुक्तम् । आर्य्य कथ्यताम् । विष्णुशर्म्मोवाच । शृणुत सम्प्रति । मित्रलाभः प्रस्तूयते यस्यायमाद्यः श्लोकः ।

असाधना वित्तहीना बुद्धिमन्तः सुहृत्तमाः ।
साधयन्त्याशु कार्य्याणि काककूर्ममृगाखुवत् ॥

The meanings of the words in these extracts are to be sought in the accompanying analytical vocabulary culled from that of Professor Johnson. The references by numbers are to Part First of these Lessons.

Exercise 35.

Translate into Sanskrit the following sentences, which involve words comprised in the foregoing extract, in addition to other words already met with in Part First;—and write also, in Sanskrit, *answers* to the questions.*

Where is the city named Pátaliputra? What city is on the bank of the Bhágíráthí? Who was Sudarśana? Where were the princes seated? How were they seated? How does the time of the wise pass away? How does the time of fools pass away?

Extract 2.

राजपुत्रा ऊचुः कथमेतत् । विष्णुशर्मा कथयति । अस्ति

* For example, in reply to the question, "How does the time of fools pass away?"—write, in Sanskrit, (as in the text,) "The time of fools passes away in dissipation, slumber, or strife."

गोदावरीतीरे विशालशाल्मलीतरुः । तत्र नानादिग्देशादागत्य पक्षिणो निवसन्ति । अथ कदाचिद् लघुपतनकनामा वायस आयान्तं पाशहस्तं व्याधमपश्यत् । तमवलोक्य तदनुसरणक्रमेण व्याकुलश्चलितः । अथ तेन व्याधेन तण्डुलकणान् विकीर्य्य जालं विस्तीर्णम् । सच प्रच्छन्नो भूत्वा स्थितः ।

Exercise 36.

What did the princes say? Where was the great silk-cotton tree? What was on the banks of the Godávarí? Who dwell in the silk-cotton tree? Having come from where? What was in the hand of the hunter? Who saw the hunter approaching? Who went after the hunter? What was done by the hunter? Who remained, having become concealed?

Extract 3.

तस्मिन्नेव काले चित्रग्रीवनामा कपोतराजः सपरिवारो वियति विसर्पंस्तांस्तण्डुलकणान् अवलोकयामास ।

The king of the pigeons warns his followers that danger lurks under the grains of rice spread out in this uninhabited quarter, and he tells them the following story, to show them the danger of yielding to the temptation of covetousness.

कपोतराजः कथयति । अहमेकदा दक्षिणारण्ये चरन्नपश्यम् । एको वृद्धव्याघ्रः स्नातः कुशहस्तः सरस्तीरे ब्रूते भो भोः पान्थ इदं सुवर्णकङ्कणं गृह्यताम् । ततो लोभाकृष्टेन केनचित् पान्थेनालोचितम् । भाग्येनैतत् सम्भवति ।

The traveller, not unnaturally, distrusts the tiger; but the tiger (by means of learned poetical quotations) dissipates his distrust; and the traveller, as directed by the tiger, goes into the lake, preparatorily to the receipt of the golden bracelet, to bathe.

ततो जातविश्वासो यावदसौ सरः स्नातुं प्रविष्टः तावदेव महापङ्के निमग्नः पलायितुमक्षमः। पङ्के पतितं दृष्ट्वा व्याघ्रो ऽवदत्। अहह महापङ्के पतितो ऽसि। अतस्त्वामुत्थापयामि। इत्युक्त्वा शनैः शनैरुपगम्य तेन व्याघ्रेण धृतः स पान्थो व्यापादितः खादितश्च।

The warning against covetousness, conveyed in this story, being thrown away upon the pigeons, they pounce down upon the rice, and are ensnared in the net. By the advice of their king (—who is too magnanimous to allude to their disregard of his previous advice—) they make a joint effort, and fly off with the net, leaving the hunter disappointed. They proceed to the abode of Hiranyaka, king of the mice, a great friend of the king of the pigeons, to whom they tell their tale, begging him to cut their snare "by the force of his teeth".

Exercise 37.

At what time did the king of the pigeons behold the grains of rice? How [in respect of his movements or his attendants] was the king of the pigeons, when he beheld the grains of rice? By the old tiger what was said? By the old tiger how circumstanced? By what was the traveller attracted? By whom was the lake entered in order to bathe? Who became immersed in a great quagmire? Having seen the traveller fallen into the quagmire, what did the tiger say? By whom was the traveller seized and devoured?

The pigeons having been freed from the net by the teeth of the mouse *Hiranyaka*, the crow, who had followed as a spectator, seeks the friendship of the mouse. The mouse is exceedingly suspicious and cautious, but the eloquence of the crow finally prevails, and they strike up a friendship. The crow takes the mouse to visit a friend of his, the tortoise *Manthara*; and, in the course of their conversation, the tortoise tells the following story illustrative of the dangers of too strong a disposition to hoard.

Extract 4.

आसीद् भैरवो नाम व्याधः। स चैकदा मांसलुब्धः धनुरादाय वनं गतः। तत्र तेन मृग एको व्यापादितः। मृगमादाय गच्छता तेन शूकरो दृष्टः। ततस्तेन मृगं भूमौ निधाय शूकरः शरेण हतः। शूकरेणाप्यागत्य स व्याधो हतश्छिन्नद्रुम इव पपात।

Exercise 38.

There was a hunter:—what was his name? Where did the hunter Bhairava go, on one occasion? Having taken what, did the hunter go to the wood? What animal was killed by him in the wood? By whom was that animal there killed? What animal was seen by him going along, he having taken up the deer? By him, having done what, was the boar smitten? By him with what was the boar smitten? Slain by the boar, like what did that hunter fall?

Extract 5.

अत्रान्तरे दीर्घरावो नाम जम्बुकस्तान् मृतान् मृगव्याधशूकरान् अपश्यत्। आलोक्याचिन्तयदसौ। अहो भाग्यं महद्भोज्यं समुपस्थितम्। भवतु। एषां मांसैर्मासत्रयं समधिकं भोजनं मे भविष्यति। ततः प्रथमबुभुक्षायामिदं निःस्वादु कोदण्डाटनीलग्नं स्नायुबन्धनं खादामि। इत्युक्त्वा तथाकरोत्। ततश्छिन्ने स्नायुबन्धने द्रुतमुत्पतितेन धनुषा हृदि भिन्नः स दीर्घरावः पञ्चत्वं गतः।

Exercise 39.

Who saw the dead deer, hunter, and boar? Having beheld, what did he think? For whom did great store of food present itself? By the flesh of whom will there be abundant food for three months? In the first desire to eat, what was first eaten by the jackal? The sinew-string being cut, who went to destruction? How so?

While the three friends dwell happily on the wooded borders of the lake, they are one day joined by a frightened deer, as the following extract tells us.

Extract 6.

अथ कदाचिच्चित्राङ्गनामा मृगः केनापि त्रासितस्तत्रागत्य मिलितः । ततः पश्चादायान्तं भयहेतुं सम्भाव्य मन्थरो जलं प्रविष्टो मूषिकश्च विवरं गत उड्डीयमानः काको वृक्षाग्रमारूढः । ततो लघुपतनकेन सुदूरं निरूप्य भयहेतुर्न कोऽप्यवलोकितः । पश्चादागत्य पुनः सर्व्वे मिलित्वोपविष्टाः । मन्थरेणोक्तम् । भद्र मृग कुशलं ते । स्वेच्छया उदकाद्याहारोऽनुभूयताम् । अत्रावस्थानेन बनमिदं सनाथीक्रियताम् । चित्राङ्गो ब्रूते । लुब्धकत्रासितोऽहं भवतां शरणमागतः ।

Exercise 40.

Who, on one occasion, having come there, met them? By whom was the deer alarmed? Having supposed a cause of alarm (to be) coming behind, what did the tortoise enter? What did the crow, flying upwards, mount upon? By the crow, having looked afar, was any cause of alarm observed? Afterwards what was said by (the tortoise) Manthara? What does (the deer) Dappled-bodied say? Who came for refuge? Frightened by whom—did the deer come for refuge?

Extract 7.

अथ मन्थरो ब्रूते । सखे मृग केन त्रासितो ऽसि । अस्मिन् निर्जने वने कदाचित् किं व्याधाः सञ्चरन्ति । मृगेणोक्तम् । अस्ति कलिङ्गविषये रुक्माङ्गदो नाम नृपतिः । स च दिग्विजयक्रमेणागत्य चन्द्रभागानदीतीरे समावासितकटको वर्त्तते । प्रातश्च तेनात्रागत्य कर्पूरसरः समीपे भवितव्यमिति व्याधानां मुखात् किम्वदन्ती श्रूयते। तदत्रापि प्रातरवस्थानं भयहेतुकमित्यालोच्य यथा कार्य्यं तथारभ्यताम् । तच्छ्रुत्वा कूर्म्मः सभयमाह । मित्र जला-शयान्तरं गच्छामि । काकमृगावपि उक्तवन्तौ । मित्र एवमस्तु ॥

Exercise 41.

What does Manthara, the tortoise, say? By whom was it said "Friend deer!—by whom wast thou alarmed?" Also, by whom was it said, "Do hunters ever roam in this uninhabited forest?" There is a king in the region of Kalinga:—what is his name? From the mouth of whom is the rumour heard? Who will go to another body of water? What two said, "Friend! —be it so?"

Extract 8.

हिरण्यको विमृश्याब्रवीत् । पुनर्जलाशये प्राप्ते मन्थरस्य कुशलम् । स्थले गच्छतो ऽस्य को विधः ।

Hiranyaka, in the course of his remonstrance, tells the following story:—

अस्ति ब्रह्मारण्ये कर्पूरतिलको नाम हस्ती । तमवलोक्य सर्वे शृगालाश्चिन्तयन्ति स्म । यद्ययं केनाप्युपायेन म्रियेत

तदास्माकमेतद्देहेन मासचतुष्टयस्य स्वेच्छाभोजनं भवेत्। ततस्तन्मध्यादेकेन वृद्धशृगालेन प्रतिज्ञा कृता । मया बुद्धिप्रभावादस्य मरणं साधयितव्यम् ।

Exercise 42

What did Hiranyaka here say? Having done what—did Hiranyaka say this? In the forest of Brahma there is an elephant:—what is his name? Having beheld that elephant, what did all the jackals think? By whom was this thought? Was the elephant, by any contrivance, destroyed? By whose contrivance was the elephant destroyed? Who was destroyed here by the contrivance of the jackal? By means of whose body may there be food for four months? Of whom may the elephant's body become the food? By whom was the promise made, viz., "The death of the elephant is to be accomplished by me—"? What was the promise of the old jackal?

Extract 9.

अनन्तरं स वञ्चकः कर्पूरतिलकसमीपं गत्वा साष्टाङ्गपातं प्रणम्योवाच । देव दृष्टिप्रसादं कुरु । हस्ती ब्रूते । कस्त्वं कुतः समायातः। सो ऽवदत् । जम्बुको ऽहम्। सर्वैर्वनवासिभिः पशुभिर्मिलित्वा भवत्सकाशं प्रस्थापितः । यद्विना राज्ञा स्थातुं न युक्तं तदत्राटवीराज्ये ऽभिषेक्तुं भवान् सर्वस्वामिगुणोपेतो निरूपितः । तद्यथा लग्नवेला न चलति सत्वरमागम्यतां देवेन इत्युक्त्वा उत्थाय चलितः ॥

Exercise 43.

Thereupon, what did that deceiver do? What was said by

the deceitful jackal? "My lord! deign the favour of a look!"—by whom was this said? What does the elephant say? "Who art thou?"—by whom was this said? "Whence hast thou come?"—by whom was this said? Who said "I am a jackal"? Is it proper, or not, to remain without a king? How did this jackal go off?

Extract 10.

ततो ऽसौ राज्यलोभाकृष्टः कर्पूरतिलकः शृगालदर्शितवर्त्मना धावन् महापङ्के निमग्नः। हस्तिनोक्तम्। सखे शृगाल किमधुना विधेयं महापङ्के पतितो ऽहम्। शृगालेन विहस्योक्तम्। देव मम पुच्छाग्रे हस्तं दत्त्वोत्तिष्ठ। ततो महापङ्के निमग्नो हस्ती शृगालैर्भक्षितः॥

Exercise 43.

By what road does the elephant, by name Karpúratilaka, go? Attracted by what does the elephant go? How does the elephant go? In what did the elephant become immersed? What was then said by the elephant? By whom was it said, "Friend jackal! what is now to be done"? By the jackal, having laughed aloud, what was then said? "Having clapped your trunk to the end of my tail, get up;"—by whom was this said? Who, and how, was then eaten by the jackals?

All the remonstrances of the deer, against the tortoise's venturing across the country to another lake, are thrown away;—for we read as follows:—

Extract 11.

ततस्तद्वचनमवधीर्य महता भयेन मन्थरो जलाश्रयमुत्सृज्य प्रचलितः। ते ऽपि हिरण्यकादयस्तमनुजग्मुः। ततः स्थले गच्छन् केनापि व्याधेन वनं पर्य्यटता स

मन्थरः प्राप्तः । सच तं गृहीत्वा उत्थाप्य धनुषि बद्धा धन्यो ऽस्मीत्यभिधाय स्वगृहाभिमुखं प्रयातः । अथ ते मृगवायसमूषिकाः परं विषादमुपगतास्तमनुगच्छन्ति स्म।

Exercise 44.

Having left what—did Manthara, the tortoise, set out? Who set out with great fear? Having disregarded the speech of the mouse, what did the tortoise do? What did Hiranyaka and the others then do? Whom did Hiranyaka and the others then follow? Was the tortoise, going along on land, caught by any one or not? By whom was the tortoise caught, going along on land? By a hunter, prowling about the forest, who was caught? Who then set out towards his home? "Fortunate am I!"—by whom was this said? Who then experienced extreme grief? Who followed the hunter?

Extract 12.

ततो बहु विलप्य हिरण्यकश्चित्राङ्गलघुपतनकावाह । यावदयं व्याधो वनान्न निःसरति तावन्मन्थरं मोचयितुं यत्नः क्रियताम् । तावूचतुः । सत्वरं यथाकार्य्यमुपदिश । हिरण्यको ब्रूते । चित्राङ्गो जलसमीपं गत्वा मृतमिव आत्मानं निश्चेष्टं दर्शयतु । काकश्च तस्योपरि स्थित्वा चञ्च्वा किमपि लिखतु । नूनमनेन लुब्धकेन मृगमांसार्थिना तत्र कच्छपं परित्यज्य सत्वरं गन्तव्यम् । ततो ऽहं मन्थरस्य बन्धनं छेत्स्यामि ।

Exercise 45.

Who said, "Let an effort be made to liberate the tortoise"? So long as the hunter does not emerge from the forest, what is to be done? Having heard this, what did those two say? Which two say—"Quickly direct how we are to act"? Having gone near the lake, what shall the deer do? Who shows himself motionless, as if dead? Having stood over whom does the crow mark him somewhat with his beak? By the hunter, desirous of flesh, what must then be done? Having quitted the tortoise, who then goes quickly near the deer? Who will cut the bonds of the tortoise? Who said, "I will cut the bonds of the tortoise"?

Extract 13.

ततश्चित्राङ्गलघुपतनकाभ्यां शीघ्रं गत्वा तथानुष्ठिते सति स व्याधः परिश्रान्तः पानीयं पीत्वा तरोरधस्तादुपविष्टः सन् तथाविधं मृगमवलोक्य कच्छपं जलसमीपे निधाय कर्त्तरिकामादाय प्रहृष्टमना मृगान्तिकं चलितः। अत्रान्तरे हिरण्यकेनागत्य छिन्नबन्धनः स कूर्म्मः सत्वरं जलाशयं प्रविष्टः सच मृग आसन्नं तं व्याधं विलोक्य उत्थाय द्रुतं पलायितः। प्रत्यावृत्य लुब्धको यावत् तरुतलमायाति तावत् कूर्म्ममपश्यन्नचिन्तयत्। उचितमेवैतत् ममासमीक्ष्यकारिणः। ततो ऽसौ निराशः कटकं प्रविष्टः। मन्थरादयश्च सर्व्वे मुक्तापदः स्वस्थानं गत्वा यथासुखमास्थिताः॥

Exercise 46.

It having been thus done by the deer and the crow, by whom were they seen? The hunter, wearied, having drunk what, sat down under a tree? Who went near the deer, having seen the deer in that condition? Having taken what—did the hunter go near the deer? Having placed the tortoise where—did the hunter go near the deer? By whom were the bonds of the tortoise cut? Having his bonds cut, what did the tortoise do? What did the deer do, having seen the hunter close at hand? Having returned, does the hunter see the tortoise or not? Not seeing the tortoise, what did the hunter think? Freed from their calamities, what did the tortoise and the others do?

The princes are of course delighted as well as edified by Vishnu Sarman's stories, and the meeting breaks up with mutual compliments. On the morrow the party re-assembles, and the Second Book of the Hitopadeśa commences as follows:—

Extract 14.

अथ राजपुत्रा ऊचुः । आर्य मित्रलाभः श्रुतस्तावद्-स्माभिः । इदानीं सुहृद्भेदं श्रोतुमिच्छामो वयम् । विष्णुशर्मोवाच । सुहृद्भेदं शृणुत यस्यायमाद्यः श्लोकः ।

वर्द्धमानो महास्नेहो मृगेन्द्रवृषयोर्वने ।
पिशुनेनातिलुब्धेन जम्बुकेन विनाशितः ॥

राजपुत्रैरुक्तम् । कथमेतत् । विष्णुशर्मा कथयति । अस्ति दक्षिणापथे सुवर्णवती नाम नगरी । तत्र वर्द्धमानो नाम बाणिजो महाजनः प्रतिवसति । तस्य प्रभूते ऽपि वित्ते ऽपरान् बन्धूनतिसमृद्धान् विलोक्य पुनरर्थवृद्धिः करणीयेति मतिर्बभूव ।

Exercise 47.

By whom was the 'Acquisition of Friends' heard? Having heard the 'Acquisition of Friends,' what do the princes desire to hear? What did Vishnuśarmma here say? To whom did Vishṇuśarmma say this? What was destroyed by a very mean greedy jackal? Where is the city called Suvarnavati? Who dwells there? Why did the merchant, though his wealth was abundant, think "yet further increase of wealth must be made"?

Extract 15.

इति सञ्चिन्त्य वर्द्धमानः सञ्जीवकनन्दकनामानौ द्वौ वृषभौ धुरि नियोज्य शकटं नानाद्रव्यपूर्णं कृत्वा वाणिज्येन काश्मीरं प्रति चलितः। अथ गच्छतस्तस्य दुर्गनाम्नि महारण्ये भग्नजानुः सञ्जीवको निपतितः। एतदवलोक्य सञ्जीवकं तत्र परित्यज्य वर्द्धमानश्चलितः। सञ्जीवकोऽपि कथं कथमपि खुरत्रये भरं कुर्वंस्तत्रैव वने स्थितः। ततो दिनेषु गच्छत्सु सञ्जीवकः स्वेच्छाहारादिलाभेन तामरण्यानीं परिभ्रमन् हृष्टपुष्टाङ्गो बलवन्ननाद।

Exercise 48.

Why did Varddhamána set out towards Caschmere? Having filled his cart with various goods, and having yoked two bullocks to the pole, who set out towards Caschmere? Why did the bullock Sanjívaka fall? Having abandoned the bullock, what did the merchant do? What was then done by the bullock? As the days went on, how did the bullock become fat and sleek in body? What did the bullock then do?

Extract 16.

तस्मिन् वने पिङ्गलकनामा सिंहः स्वभुजोपार्ज्जितराज्यसुखमनुभवन्नास्ते। सचैकदा पिपासाकुलितः पानीयं पातुं यमुनाकच्छमगमत्। तेनच तत्र सिंहेनाननुभूतपूर्व्वकं प्रलयघनगर्ज्जितमिव सञ्जीवकनर्दितमश्रावि। तच्छ्रुत्वासौ पानीयमपीत्वा सचकितं परिवृत्य स्वस्थानमागत्य किमिदमित्यालोच्य तूष्णीं स्थितः। सच तथाविधः करटकदमनकाभ्यां तन्मन्त्रिपुत्राभ्यां शृगालाभ्यां

दृष्टः। तं तथाविधं दृष्ट्वा दमनकः करटकमाह। सखे करटक किमित्युदकार्थी स्वामी पानीयमपीत्वा मन्दं मन्दमवतिष्ठते। करटको ब्रूते। मित्र दमनक मम सम्मतेनास्य सेवैव न क्रियते। तत् किमस्य चेष्टानिरूपणेन। यतो ऽनेन राज्ञा ऽवधीरिताभ्यामावाभ्यां महद्दुःखमनुभूतम्।

Exercise 49.

Where did the lion, Pingalaka, go to drink water? Why did he do so? What was then heard by the lion? Having heard that great sound, what did the lion do? Who remained silently, thinking "What is this"? By whom was the lion, in that condition, seen? What did Damanaka then say? Who said, "Not with my consent is even this service performed"? Whose service? Why is the service of the lion not, with his own consent, performed by the jackal Karataka?

In illustration of the danger of being officious in serving a superior, Karataka tells the following story:—

Extract 17.

अस्ति वाराणस्यां कर्पूरपटो नाम रजकः। सचैकदा निर्भरं प्रसुप्तः। तदनन्तरं द्रव्याणि हर्त्तुं तद्गृहं चौरः प्रविष्टः। तस्य प्राङ्गणे गर्द्दभो बद्धस्तिष्ठति। कुक्कुरश्चोपविष्टः। तं चौरमवलोक्य गर्द्दभः श्वानमाह। भवतो ऽयं व्यापारः। तत् किमिति त्वमुच्चैः शब्दं कृत्वा स्वामिनं न जागरयसि। कुक्कुरो ब्रूते। नियोगस्यास्य चिन्ता त्वया न कार्य्या। त्वमेव जानासि यथाहमस्य गृहरक्षां करोमि। यतो ऽयं चिरान्निर्वृतो ममोपयोगं न जानाति। तेन-

धुना ममाहारदाने ऽपि मन्दादरः। विना विधुरादर्शनं स्वामिनो ऽनुजीविषु मन्दादरा भवन्ति। ततो गर्द्दभः सकोपमाह। अाः पापीयांस्त्वं यः स्वामिकार्य्यमुपेक्षसे ...

Exercise 50.

Who entered the house of the washerman, and for what purpose? Who stands bound in the courtyard of the washerman? Whom did the donkey address, having beheld the thief? What did the donkey say to the dog? What does the dog (in reply) say? Who said "Thou thyself knowest how I perform the washerman's house-watching"? Who is now neglectful in the bestowal of food? Without what do masters become deficient in respect towards their attendants? What does the donkey do in order that the master may awake? Who made an excessive screeching? What does the washerman, awakened by that screeching, do?

The jackal, Damanaka (—himself no paragon of virtue—), shocked at the principles enunciated by his brother, Karataka, resolves to wait upon the king, and attempt to discover the cause of his disquietude.

Extract 18.

ततो दमनको विस्मित इव पिङ्गलकसमीपं गतः। अथ दूरादेव राज्ञा दृष्टः सादरं प्रवेशितस्तं साष्टाङ्गं प्रणम्योपविष्टः। राजाह। चिरादृष्टो ऽसि। दमनको ब्रूते।

यद्यपि मया सेवकेन श्रीमद्देवपादानां न किञ्चित् प्रयोजनमस्ति तथापि प्राप्तकाले ऽनुजीविना सान्निध्यमवश्यं कर्त्तव्यमित्यागतो ऽस्मि ।

Exercise 51.

How did the jackal, Damanaka, go to the lion, Pingalaka? Was the jackal seen by the lion or not? What did the king then say? Has the king any occasion for a servant? If the king has no occasion for a servant, then what is the use of Damanaka's coming? What does the jackal say here (—or in regard to this point)? When must attendance necessarily be made by a retainer? By whom must attendance necessarily be made when the time (or a fit occasion) has arrived? By whom was this assertion made? To whom was this assertion made by the jackal?

The lion-king and Damanaka, the jackal, have a long conversation, and Damanaka gets into great favour at court. But he thereupon becomes about as selfish as his brother; and, on his return from his audience, he narrates a story with much the same moral as that which his brother had narrated. It here follows.

Extract 18.

अस्त्युत्तरापथे अर्बुदशिखरनाम्नि पर्व्वते महाविक्रमो नाम सिंहः । तस्य पर्व्वतकन्दरमधिशयानस्य केशराग्रं मूषिकः कश्चिच्छिनत्ति । स सिंहः केशराग्रं लूनं बुद्ध्वा कुपितो विवरान्तर्गतं मूषिकमलभमानो ऽचिन्तयत् । किं विधेयमत्र । ततो ग्रामं गत्वा दधिकर्णनामा विडालो मांसाद्याहारेण सन्तोष्य प्रयत्नादानीय स्वकन्दरे धृतः । ततस्तद्भयान्मूषिको वहिर्न निःसरति । तेनासौ सिंहो ऽक्षतकेशरः सुखं स्वपिति । मूषिकशब्दं यदा यदा शृणोति

तदा तदा सविशेषं तं विडालं मांसाहारदानेन संवर्द्ध-
यति। अथैकदा स मूषिकः क्षुधापीडितो बहिः सञ्चरंस्तेन
मार्जारेण प्राप्तो व्यापादितः खादितश्च। अनन्तरं स सिंहो
यदा कदाचिदपि मूषिकशब्दं न शुश्राव तदोपयोगाभा-
वात् तस्य विडालस्याहारदाने मन्दादरो बभूव ॥

Exercise 52.

Who nibbles the ends of the mane of the lion sleeping in the cave of the mountain? What did the lion think, having perceived the ends of his mane nibbled? Not catching the mouse, which had gone into its hole, is the lion angry or not? Having gone to the village, what does the lion do? Does the mouse then, for fear of the cat, come out? How does the lion sleep, when his hairs are not injured? Whenever the lion hears the sound of the mouse then what does he do? Why does the mouse, on one occasion, come out? Coming out, by whom is the mouse caught? And further, when the lion never heard the sound of the mouse then what did he do?

Damanaka, however, sticks to his plan of acting towards the king as loyally as he conveniently can,—due regard being had to his own interests;—and at his next audience he finds occasion to tell the king the following story?

Extract 19.

अस्ति श्रीपर्वतमध्ये ब्रह्मपुराख्यं नगरम्। अत्र शैल-
शिखरे घण्टाकर्णो नाम राक्षसः प्रतिवसतीति जनप्रवादः
श्रूयते। एकदा घण्टामादाय पलायमानः कश्चिच्चौरो
व्याघ्रेण व्यापादितः। तत्पाणिपतिता घण्टा वानरैः
प्राप्ता। ते वानरास्तां घण्टामनुक्षणं वादयन्ति। ततो
नगरजनैर्मनुष्यः खादितो दृष्टः प्रतिक्षणं घण्टारावश्च

श्रूयते । अनन्तरं घण्टाकर्णः कुपितो मनुष्यान् खादति घण्टाञ्च वादयति इत्युक्त्वा जनाः सर्व्वे नगरात् पलायिताः । ततः करालया नाम वृद्धया विमृश्य मर्कटा घण्टां वादयन्ति स्वयं विज्ञाय राजा विज्ञापितः । देव यदि कियद्धनोपक्षयः क्रियते तदाहमेनं घण्टाकर्णं साधयामि । ततो राज्ञा तुष्टेन तस्यै धनं दत्तम् । वृद्धयाच मण्डलं कृत्वा तत्र गणेशादिगौरवं दर्शयित्वा स्वयं वानरप्रियफलान्यादाय वनं प्रविश्य फलान्याकीर्णानि । ततो घण्टां परित्यज्य वानराः फलासक्ता बभूवुः । वृद्धाच घण्टां गृहीत्वा नगरमागता सकललोकपूज्या ऽभवत् ।

Exercise 53.

Where does the demon Ghaṇṭákarṇa dwell? What popular rumour is heard in the city called Brahmapura? Having seized a bell, who, fleeing, was killed by a tiger? By whom was the bell, fallen from his hand, found? Who then rings that bell every moment? By whom was the man seen eaten? And what is heard every moment? All the people, having said what, fled from the city? By whom, having discerned the state of the case, was the king counselled? Who said, "I will settle this demon, Ghaṇṭákarṇa"? To the old woman what was given by the king well-pleased? By the old woman what was then done? Having seen the fruits, what was done by the monkeys? Having picked up the bell, what did the old woman become?

Eventually the jackals, claiming much credit for their diplomacy, introduce the bullock to the lion, who takes a great liking to him. Thereupon, naturally, the jackals become envious, and the 'Separation of the Friends,' the business of Book Second, is entered upon.

Extract 20.

तदाह दमनकः । किमत्र विधेयम् । आत्मकृतोऽयं दोषः। स्वयङ्कृतेऽपि दोषे परिदेवनमप्यनुचितम्। स्वयङ्कृतो यं दोषः अत्र विलपनमनुचितम्। क्षणं विमृश्य। मित्र सहसैव यथाऽनयोः सौहार्द्दं मया कारितं तथा भेदोऽपि कार्य्यः। करटको ब्रूते । अस्त्वेवं किन्त्वनयोर्महान् नैसर्गिकः स्नेहः कथं भेदयितुं शक्यः । दमनक आह। उपायश्चिन्तनीयः।

तथाचोक्तम्।

उपायेन हि यच्छक्यं न तच्छक्यं पराक्रमैः।
काकी कनकसूत्रेण कृष्णसर्पमघातयत् ॥

करटकः पृच्छति। कथमेतत्। दमनकः कथयति। कस्मिंश्चित् तरौ वायसदम्पती निवसतः । तयोश्चापत्यानि तरुकोटरावस्थितकृष्णसर्पेण खादितानि । ततः वायसी ब्रूते स्वामिन् त्यज्यतामयं तरुः। अत्र यावत् कृष्णसर्पस्तावदावयोः सन्ततिः कदाचिदपि न भविष्यति। यतः।

दुष्टा भार्य्या शठं मित्रं भृत्यश्चोत्तरदायकः।
ससर्पे च गृहे वासो मृत्युरेव न संशयः॥

Exercise 54.

"What is to be done here?"—who says that? By whom was said, "This is a fault committed by myself"? Where the fault is one's own doing, is complaint proper or not? Where is lamentation improper? Having reflected for a moment, what does Damanaka say? How is it possible to divide (or estrange from one another) those of whom there is a great natural affection? Who says—"An expedient is to be thought of"? Is all that possible by means of force, which is possible by means of expedients? Who killed a black snake by means of a golden necklace? Where do the crow and his mate dwell? By whom were the crow's young one's eaten? Why does the female crow say—"My lord, let this tree be quitted"? Is there any doubt that dwelling in a house where there are snakes, is death simply? What-like is a servant who gives (pert) answers? What else (besides these, is entitled to be called) death simply?

Extract 21.

वायसो ब्रूते । प्रिये न भेतव्यम् । वारं वारं मयैतस्य महापराधः सोढः । इदानीं पुनर्न क्षन्तव्यः । वायस्याह कथमनेन बलवता कृष्णसर्पेन सार्द्धं भवान् विग्रहयितुं समर्थः । वायसो ब्रूते । अलमनया चिन्तया । यतः ।

बुद्धिर्यस्य बलं तस्य निर्बुद्धेस्तु कुतो बलम् ।
पश्य सिंहो महोन्मत्तः शशकेन निपातितः ॥

वायस्याह । कथमेतत् । वायसः कथयति ।

Exercise 55.

Who says—"My dear (wife), it is not to be feared? Whose great offence had been again and again borne by the crow? Is the black snake again to be forgiven? Is the crow able to contend with a powerful black snake, or not? "Enough, (or have done) with this anxiety"—by whom was this said? If strength belongs to him who has intellect, then whence (should be) any strengh of the unintelligent? What sort of lion was killed by the rabbit? Of the very headstrong lion, killed by the rabbit, by whom was the story told?

Extract 22.

अस्ति मन्दरनाम्नि पर्व्वते दुर्दान्तो नाम सिंहः । सच सर्व्वदा पशूनां बधं विदधान एवास्ते । ततः सर्व्वैः पशुभिर्मेलकं कृत्वा स सिंहो विज्ञप्तः । देव किमर्थं सर्व्वपशुबधः क्रियते । वयमेव भवदाहारार्थं प्रत्यहमेकैकं पशुमुपढौकयामः । सिंहेनोक्तम् । यद्येतदभिमतं भवतां तर्हि भवतु । ततःप्रभृति प्रत्यहमेकैकं पशुमुपकल्पितं भक्षयन्नास्ते । अथ कदाचित् कस्यापि वृद्धशशकस्य वासरः प्राप्तः । ततः सो ऽचिन्तयत् । त्रासहेतोर्व्विनीतिस्तु क्रियते जीविताशया । पञ्चत्वं चेद्गमिष्यामि किं सिंहानुनयेन मे ॥ तन्मन्दं मन्दमुपगच्छामि । ततः सिंहो ऽपि क्षुधापीडितः कोपात् तमुवाच । कुतस्त्वं विलम्बादागतो ऽसि । शशको ऽब्रवीत् । नाहमपराद्धः पथि सिंहान्तरेण बलाद्धृतः । तस्याग्रे पुनरागमनाय शपथं कृत्वा स्वामिनं निवेदयितुमत्रागतो ऽस्मि ।

Exercise 56.

In what mountain docs the lion, named Durdánta, live? Who remains always, in the mountain named Mandara, perpetrating the slaughter of the beasts? Having made a meeting, what was done by all the beasts? "My lord,—why is the slaughter of all the beasts made?"—by whom was this asked? Who (will undertake to) supply a separate beast daily for the food of the lion? "If such be the choice of you, Sirs, then be it so,"—by whom was this said? And to whom was this said? Thenceforward who continues eating each day the beast assigned? Of whom, on one occasion, did the turn (to be eaten) arrive? Having seen his own turn arrived, what did the old rabbit think? By him who has hopes of life, (in respect) of whom is submissiveness made (or shown)? "What have *I* to do with conciliating the lion?"—by whom was this said? Who will here go to destruction (—a resolution into the five elements, earth, water, air, fire, ether—)? Who approaches the lion very leisurely? What did the lion say to him? Did the lion, pained with hunger, address him with anger, or not? What did the rabbit say?

Extract 23.

सिंहः सकोपमाह। सत्वरं गत्वा मां दर्शय क्वासौ दुरात्मा तिष्ठति। ततः शशकस्तं गृहीत्वा गम्भीरकूपसमीपमागतः। अत्रागत्य पश्यतु स्वामीत्युक्त्वा तस्मिन् कूपजले तस्यैव प्रतिबिम्बं दर्शितवान् । ततो ऽसौ दर्पाध्मातस्तस्योपरि आत्मानं निक्षिप्य पञ्चत्वं गतः । अतो ऽहं ब्रवीमि बुद्धिर्यस्य इत्यादि। वायसी ब्रूते । श्रुतं मया। कर्त्तव्यतां ब्रूहि। वायसो ऽवदत् । प्रिये आसन्ने सरसि राजपुत्रः सततामागत्य स्नाति। तस्मिन् प्रस्तरे तदङ्गादवतारितं कनकसूत्रं चञ्च्वा धृत्वानीयास्मिन् कोटरे धरिष्यसि। अथ कदाचित् कनकसूत्रं दृषदि संस्थाप्य स्नातुं प्रविष्टे राजपुत्रे वायस्या तदनुष्ठितम् । अथ कनकसूत्रानुसरणप्रवृत्तैः राजपुरुषैः कोटरे निरूप्यमाणः कृष्णसर्पो व्यापादितः । अतो ऽहं ब्रवीमि। उपायेन हि यच्छक्यमित्यादि। करटक आह। यद्येवं तदा गच्छ पन्थानः सन्तु ते शिवाः।

Exercise 57.

How (or in what mood of mind) did the lion say, "Having gone quickly, show me where that base-souled one abides"?

Having taken the lion, near what did the rabbit come? Having come there, what does the rabbit say? In the water of the well, what did the rabbit point out? Then how did the lion go to destruction? Having heard this, what does the female crow say? "Tell thou what is to be done,"—by whom was this said? Who bathes in the neighbouring lake? From whose person was a golden chain put off, at the time of bathing? Having seized the gold chain in her beak, where shall the female crow place it? Having placed the gold chain upon what—did the prince go in to bathe? Then by whom was that accomplished (which had been directed by the crow)? By whom was the black snake killed? "May thy paths be prosperous!"—by whom was this said, and to whom?

Damanaka goes to Pingalaka and succeeds in raising suspicions of intended treachery on the part of the ox—whereupon the lion kills the blameless bullock; and thus is effected 'The Separation of Friends.' We proceed to

THE THIRD BOOK, ON WAR.

Extract 24.

पुनः कथारम्भकाले राजपुत्रैरुक्तम् । आर्य्य राजपुत्रा वयं तद्विग्रहं श्रोतुं नः कुतूहलमस्ति । विष्णुशर्म्मोवाच । यदेव भवद्भ्यो रोचते तत्कथयामि । विग्रहः श्रूयतां यस्यायमाद्यः श्लोकः ।

हंसैः सह मयूराणां विग्रहे तुल्यविक्रमे
विश्वास्य वञ्चिताः हंसाः काकैः स्थित्वारिमन्दिरे ॥

Exercise 58.

Of whom is it a pleasure to hear of war? By whom was this said? At what time was this said? What did Vishnuśarma then say? "Just what is relished by you, Sirs, that I relate,"—by whom was this said? "Let war be heard,"—by whom was this said? To whom was it said? By whom, having stayed in the abode of the enemy, were the swans deceived? Having trusted whom—were the swans deceived? What sort of war was that of the peacocks with the swans?

Extract 25.

अस्ति नर्मदातीरे पर्व्वतोपत्यकायां विशालः शाल्मलीतरुः। तत्र निर्मितनीडक्रोडे पक्षिणः सुखेन वर्षास्वपि निवसन्ति। अथ नीलपटलैरिव जलपटलावृते नभस्तले धारासारैर्महती वृष्टिर्बभूव। ततो वानरांस्तत्तरुतले ऽवस्थितान् शीतार्त्तान् कम्पमानानवलोक्य पक्षिभिरुक्तम्। भो भो वानराः श्रूयताम्।

अस्माभिर्निर्मिता नीडाश्चञ्चुमात्राहृतैस्तृणैः।
हस्तपादादिसंयुक्ता यूयं किमवसीदथ॥

तच्छ्रुत्वा वानरैर्जातामर्षैरालोचितम्। अहो निर्वातनीडगर्भावस्थिताः सुखिनः पक्षिणो ऽस्मान् निन्दन्ति। तद्भवतु तावद्वृष्टेरुपशमः। अनन्तरं शान्ते पानीयवर्षे तैर्वानरैर्वृक्षमारुह्य सर्व्वे नीडा भग्नाः। तेषां पक्षिणामण्डानि चाधः पातितानि॥

Exercise 59.

On what part (—in what place—) of the mountain was the large silk-cotton tree? Even at what time do the birds dwell there with comfort? In the hollow of the nests formed there, who dwell comfortably? What sort of shower at that time took place? With what was the face (—surface—) of the sky overspread? Who then stood, pained by the cold, at the foot of that tree? Having beheld the monkeys shivering, what was said by the birds? How were the nests of the birds constructed? Are the birds possessed of hands, &c.? Who are possessed of hands, &c.? Having heard the speech of the birds, what was thought by the monkeys? Whom do the birds blame? "Let there only be a cessation of the rain"—by whom was this said? By the monkeys, having ascended the tree, what was done?

Extract 26.

अस्ति शृगालः कश्चित् स्वेच्छया नगरोपान्ते भ्रमन् नीलसन्धानभाण्डे निपतितः। पश्चादुत्थातुमसमर्थः प्रातरात्मानं मृतवत् सन्दर्श्य स्थितः। अथ नीलीभाण्डस्वामिना ऽसावुत्थाप्य दूरे नीत्वा परित्यक्तः। ततो ऽसौ वनं गत्वात्मानं नीलवर्णमवलोक्याचिन्तयत्। अहमिदानीं उत्तमवर्णस्तदात्मनः किमुत्कर्षं न साधयामि। इत्युक्त्वा शृगालानाहूय तेनोक्तम्। अहं भगवत्या वनदेवतया स्वहस्तेनारण्यराज्ये सर्व्वौषधिरसेनाभिषिक्तः। पश्यन्तु मम वर्णम्। तदद्यारभ्य अस्मदाज्ञया ऽस्मिन्नारण्ये व्यवहारः कार्य्यः। शृगालाश्च तं विशिष्टवर्णमवलोक्य साष्टाङ्गपातं प्रणम्योचुः। यथाज्ञापयति देव इत्यनेन क्रमेण सर्व्वेष्वरण्यवासिष्वाधिपत्यं तस्य बभूव ततस्तेन स्वज्ञातिभिरावृतेनाधिक्यं साधितम्।

Exercise 60.

Who fell into the indigo-vat? Being unable to get up (—out—) again, what was done by the jackal? Who remained, having shown himself as one dead? In the morning what was done by the owner of the indigo-vat? What was then done by the jackal? Who, having gone to the forest, said, "I am now of the finest colour"? What else was said by the jackal? (According to his own account) by whom, and by means of what, was the jackal inaugurated in the empire of the forest? "Let the jackals behold my colour!"—by whom was this said? What therefore (—according to the jackal—) is to be done, from this day forward? Having made obeisance with a prostration of the eight members of the body, what did the jackals say? Why did the jackals say this? Of whom, over all the inhabitants of the forest, did the sovereignty become (established)? His superiority having been established, by whom was the jackal surrounded (or attended)?

Extract 27.

ततस्तेन सिंहव्याघ्रादीनुत्तमपरिजनान् प्राप्य शृगालानवलोक्य लज्जमानेनावज्ञाय दूरीकृताः स्वज्ञातयः । ततो विषण्णान् शृगालानवलोक्य वृद्धशृगालेन प्रतिज्ञातम् । मा विषीदत चेदनेनानीतिज्ञेन वयं मर्म्मज्ञाः परिभूताः । तद्यथा ऽयं नश्यति तन्मया विधेयम् । यतो ऽत्र व्याघ्रादयो वर्णमात्रविप्रलब्धा । शृगालमज्ञात्वा राजानममं मन्यन्ते । तद्यथायं परिचीयते तत्कुरुत । तत्रैवमनुष्ठेयं यथा वदामि । सर्व्वे सन्ध्यासमये तत्सन्निधाने महारावमेकदा करिष्यथ । ततस्तं शब्दमाकर्ण्य स्वभावात् तेनापि शब्दः कर्त्तव्यः । यतः ।

य स्वभावो हि यस्य स्यात् तस्यासौ दुरतिक्रमः ।
श्वा यदि क्रियते राजा स किं न श्नात्युपनहम् ॥

ततः शब्दाद्विज्ञाय व्याघ्रेण हन्तव्यः । तथा ऽनुष्ठिते सति तद् वृत्तम् ॥

Exercise 61.

By whom were lions, tigers, and other pre-eminent courtiers obtained? By the jackal—having done what? Again—having done what? What was then promised by an old jackal? By an old jackal—having beheld what—was this promised? By what were the tigers, &c. deceived? Not having known what—do they (the tigers, &c.) suppose this (one) a king? In order that this may be understood, what is to be done? Having heard the voice of the jackals, what was done by the jackal? It having been thus carried out, what took place?

Extract 28.

अस्त्ययोध्यायां पुरि चूडामणिर्नाम क्षत्रियः । तेन धनार्थिना कायक्लेशेन भगवांश्चन्द्रार्द्धचूडामणिश्चिरमाराधितः । ततः क्षीणपापो ऽसौ स्वप्ने दर्शनं लब्ध्वा भगवतः प्रसादाद्यक्षेश्वरेणादिष्टः । त्वमद्य प्रातरेव क्षौरं कारयित्वा लगुडहस्तः सन् स्वगृहद्वारि निभृतं स्थास्यसि । ततो यमेवागतं भिक्षुकं प्राङ्गणे पश्यसि तं निर्दयं लगुडप्रहारेण हनिष्यसि । ततो ऽसौ भिक्षुकः तत्क्षणात् सुवर्णपूर्णकलशो भविष्यति । तेन त्वं यावज्जीवं सुखी भविष्यसि । तदनन्तरं तदनुष्ठिते सति तद्वृत्तम् । ततः क्षौरकरणायानीतेन नापितेन तत्सर्व्वमालोक्य चिन्तितम् । अहो निधिप्राप्तेरयमुपायः । तदहमप्येवं किं न करोमि । ततःप्रभृति स नापित प्रतिदिनं तथाविधलगुडहस्तः भिक्षुकागमनमपेक्षते । एकदा तेन तथा प्राप्तो भिक्षुको लगुडेन हत्वा व्यापादितः । तेनापराधेन सो ऽपि नापितो राजपुरुषैस्ताडितः पञ्चत्वं गतः ॥

Exercise 62.

By the Kshatriya, named Chúdámani, in the city (of) Ayodhyá, what vision was obtained in a dream? With club in hand, and having done what, does the Kshatriya stand at the door of his own house? Whom shall the Kshatriya pitilessly kill by a blow of the club? Struck by the club, what does the beggar instantly become? Having witnessed all that, what was thought by the barber? "Hallo! *This* is the way to gain treasure!"—by whom was this said? Why then does he not do the same? Thenceforth what does that barber do? By whom, on one occasion, was a beggar killed?

The Fourth and concluding book of the Hitopadeśa is devoted to the subject of 'Peace.' It opens as follows:—

Extract 29.

पुनः कथारम्भकाले राजपुत्रैरुक्तम् । आर्य्य विग्रहः श्रुतोऽस्माभिः । सन्धिरधुनाभिधीयताम् । विष्णुशर्म्मणोक्तम् । श्रूयताम् । सन्धिमपि कथयामि यस्यायमाद्यश्लोकः ।

वृत्ते महति सङ्ग्रामे राज्ञोर्निहतसेनयोः ।
स्थेयाभ्यां गृध्रचक्राभ्यां वाचा सन्धिः कृतः क्षणात् ॥

Exercise 63.

War having been heard, what is now to be told? When was this said, and by whom? Who gives an account of peace also? A great battle having taken place, what was then done? By whom was peace made on the moment?

From Book Fourth we select two stories, one of which, if the reader has read the Arabian Nights' Entertainments, may remind him of Alnascar; while the other is the Indian original of the pathetic Welsh ballad of "Beth Gellert." The Hitopadeśa —itself a compilation—) is interesting as being the ancient store-house of Apologue—the store-house on which hundreds of subsequent writers have indented, with or without acknowledgment, —usually without.

Extract 30.

अस्ति देवीकोट्टनगरे देवशर्मा नाम ब्राह्मणः । तेन विषुवत्सङ्क्रान्तौ शक्तुपूर्णशरावः प्राप्तः । ततस्तमादायासौ भाण्डपूर्णकुम्भकारमण्डपिकायां रौद्रेणाकुलितः सुप्तः । ततः शक्तुरक्षार्थं हस्ते दण्डमादायाचिन्तयत् । यद्यहमिमं शक्तुशरावं विक्रीय दश कपर्दकान् प्राप्नोमि तदा तैरिह-समये कपर्दकैर्घटशरावादिकमुपक्रीय अनेकधा वृद्धैस्तै-र्धनैः पुनः पुनः पूगवस्त्रादिकमुपक्रीय विक्रीय बाणिज्यं कृत्वा लक्षसङ्ख्यकधनान्युत्पाद्य विवाहचतुष्टयं करोमि । ततस्तासु पत्नीषु या रूपयौवनवती तस्यामधिकानुरागं करोमि । तदनन्तरं सञ्जातेर्ष्यास्ताः सपत्न्य अन्योन्यं यदा द्वन्द्वं करिष्यन्ति तदा ऽहं कोपाकुलः सर्वाः सपत्नीर्लगुडेन ताडयिष्यामि । इत्यभिधाय तेन लगुडः प्रक्षिप्तः शक्तुश-रावश्चूर्णितो भाण्डानिच भग्नानि । ततो भग्नभाण्डश्रव-णादागत्य कुम्भकारेण गले हस्तं दत्त्वा मण्डपिकाद्ब-हिःकृतः ॥

Exercise 64.

By whom was a platter-full of meal found? By him who found the platter-full of meal what was done? Why did the Bráhman lie down to sleep? What was then thought by the Bráhman? "I will beat all the rival wives with a club,"—by whom was this said? On the hearing of the sound of the broken vessels, what was then done by the potter?

Extract 31.

अस्त्युज्जयिन्यां माधवो नाम ब्राह्मणः । तस्य ब्राह्मणी बालापत्यरक्षार्थं ब्राह्मणमवस्थाप्य स्नातुं गता । अथ ब्राह्मणस्य कृते राज्ञः पार्व्वणश्राद्धं दातुमागतो जनः । तं दृष्ट्वा ब्राह्मणः सहजदारिद्र्यादचिन्तयत् । यदि सत्वरं न गच्छामि तदा ऽन्यः कश्चिच्छ्राद्धं ग्रहीष्यति । शिशोश्चात्र रक्षकः को ऽपि नास्ति तत् किं करोमि । यातु । चिरकालपालितममुं सुतनिर्विशेषं नकुलं बालकरक्षार्थं व्यवस्थाप्य गच्छामि । तथा कृत्वा गतः । ततस्तेन नकुलेन बालकसमीपमागच्छन् तूष्णीं कृष्णसर्पो व्यापादितः खण्डितश्च । अथासौ नकुलो ब्राह्मणमायान्तमवलोक्य रक्तविलिप्तमुखपादः सत्वरमुपागत्य ब्राह्मणस्य चरणयोर्लुलोठ । ततो ऽसौ ब्राह्मणस्तं तथाविधं दृष्ट्वा मम पुत्रो ऽनेन भक्षित इत्यविचार्य्य तं व्यापादितवान् । अनन्तरं यावदुपसृत्य पश्यति ब्राह्मणस्तावद्बालकः सुस्थः स्वपिति सर्पस्तु व्यापादितस्तिष्ठति । ततो ऽसौ ब्राह्मणो विषादमुपगतः ॥

Exercise 65.

Having appointed whom to guard the child, did the Bráhmaṉ woman go to bathe? Why did the Bráhmaṉ reflect, "If I do not go quickly, then some other one will obtain this wealth"? In the absence of the Bráhmaṉ, who is the protector of the child? By whom was the black-snake* killed?

* The "black-snake," like the "black-bird," has (—as denoted by the compound word—) a special and restricted meaning. As the "black-bird" is only the songster, and not the crow,—so the "black-snake" is the deadly "Cobra Capello," and no other black-coloured serpent.

ABBREVIATIONS USED IN THE VOCABULARY.

ins., instrumental, or 3d case. (Nos. 50, 113, 115, and 116.)

loc., locative, or 7th case. (Nos. 113, &c.)

du., dual. (Nos. 104 and 106.)

cr., crude or uninflected state. (No. 1, p. 3).

s., substantive.

vb. verb.

par., *parasmai-pada*. (This is the technical name of the tense-affixes, of the active voice, exhibited under No. 118. For an explanation of the name, see under *átm.*—here following.)

átm., *átmane-pada*. (No. 91. *Parasmai-pada* means 'an expression for another,' and *átmane-pada* means 'an expression for one's self'. The *átm.* affixes are therefore analagous to those of the Greek Middle. They are exhibited in the Vocabulary under the word ब्रूते *brúte.*)

cl., class or conjugation. (Nos. 15, 93, and 96—103.)

caus., causal form. This form is very similar to that of the 10th cl. (See No. 103.)

agt., agent, noun of agency, or verbal adjective.

pot., potential. (No. 133.)

ind. pret. part., indeclinable preterite participle, or *conjunctive* participle. (See No. 59, and also, in the Vocabulary, under the word अवलोक्य *avalokya*).

rt., verbal root. (No. 13.)

Dwan., *Dwandwa* compound. (Nos. 104, 105.)

Bahu., *Bahuvríhi* compound. (No. 107.)

Tat., *Tatpurusha* compound. (No. 108.)

Karm., *Karmadháraya* compound (No. 69.)

VOCABULARY, SANSKRIT AND ENGLISH.

अ *a.*

अकरवम् 1*st per. sin.* 1*st pret. of the vb.* कृ 8*th cl. par.* Do, make. अकरोत् 3*d pers. sin.*

अक्षत *pass. part.* (*of the vb.* क्षण, Kill, injure, *with* अ *priv.*) Uninjured.

अक्षमः *nom. sin. m. of* अक्षम *adj.* Unable.

अगमत् 3*d pers. sin.* 3*d pret. of the vb.* गम 1*st cl. par.* Go.

अग्र *s. n.* The front, point, extremity. अग्रे *loc. ind.* Before, in presence of.

अघातयत् 3*d pers. sin.* 1*st pret. of* घाति (*causal form of the vb.* हन, slay), He caused to be killed.

अङ्ग *s. n.* A limb, member. The body.

अचिन्तयत् 3*d pers. sin.* 1*st pret. of the vb.* चित (इ) 10*th cl. par.* Think, reflect.

अटनी *s. f.* The notched extremity of a bow.

अटवी *s. f.* A wood, forest.

अण्ड *s. n.* An egg. अण्डानि *nom. or acc. pl.*

अतस् *ind.* From this. Than this. Hence, hereafter. On this account.

अतीव *ind.* Excessively, very much.

अत्र *ind.* Here.

अत्रान्तरे *ind.* Thereupon. In the meanwhile.

अथ *an inceptive particle.* After. Then. Now. And. But.

अदृष्ट *pass. part.* (*of the vb.* दृश see, *with* अ *priv.*) Unseen.

अद्य *ind.* Now, to-day.

अद्यारभ्य *ind.* Commencing to-day, from this day forwards.

अधस् *ind.* Down, below.

अधस्तात् *ind.* Below, at the bottom.

अधिकः *nom. sin. m. of adj.* Exceeding, more, additional.

अधिशयान *pres. part. of the vb.* शी 2*d cl. átm.* Lie down,—*with* अधि, Inhabit.—नस्य *gen. sin. m.*

अधुना *ind.* Now, at present.

अननुभूत *pass. part.* (*of the vb.* भू, Be, *with prep.* अनु *and* अन्) Unperceived.

अनन्तरम् *ind.* Immediately, afterwards.

अनया *ins. sing. f. of* इदम् *pron.* This.—अनयोः *gen. du. m.*

अनीतिज्ञ Impolitic, silly.

अनुक्षणम् *ind.* Every instant, continually.

अनुगच्छति *3d pers. sin. pres.* (*of the vb.* गम 1*st cl. par.* Go, *with* अनु, After) Follows.

अनुचितम् *nom. sin. n. adj.* Improper.

अनुजग्मुः *3d pers. pl. 2d pret. par.* (*of the vb.* गम Go, *with* अनु, After.) They followed.

अनुजीविन् *agt.* A follower, dependant.

अनुनय *s. m.* Civility.

अनुभवद्भिः *ins. pl. m.* By those enjoying or experiencing.

अनुभूत *pass. part.* Experienced, felt.

अनुभूयताम् *3d pers. sin. imp. pass.* (No. 132, *of the vb.* भू, Be, *with* अनु, No. 130.) Let it be enjoyed.

अनुरागः *nom. sin. s. m.* Love, affection.

अनुष्ठिते *loc. sin. n.* Done, executed.

अनुष्ठेयम् *fut. pass. part.* (*of the vb.* ष्ठा *with* अनु.) To be done, or accomplished.

अनुसरण *s. n.* A following, a going after.

अनेकधा *ind.* In many ways.

अनेन *ins. sin. m.* or *n.* (*of* इदम् *pron.*) By or with this, him, or it.

अन्तर् *ind.* Inwardly, within.

अन्तरम् *nom. or acc. sin. of* अन्तर *s. n.* Interval, distance, difference. *At the end of a word it may be rendered by* Another; *as* देशान्तर, Another country; पुरुषान्तर, Another man.

अन्तर्गत *pass. part.* Gone within, included in.

अन्तिकम् *ind.* Near.

अन्योन्यम् *ind.* One with another, mutually.

अपत्यम् *nom. sin. s. n.* Offspring.

अपरान् *acc. pl. of* अपर. Other.

अपराद्ध *adj.* Culpable.

अपश्यन् *nom. sin.* Not seeing. Nos. 125 *and* 38.

अपश्यम् *1st pers. sin. 1st. pret.* (*of the vb.* दृश 1*st cl. par.*) I saw.

अब्रवीत् *3d pers. sin. 1st pret. of the vb* ब्रू *2d cl. par.* Say, speak.

अभिधाय *ind. pret. part.* (*of the vb.* धा, Hold, *with* अभि.) Having said, or called out.

अभिमतम् *nom. sin. n.* Wished, approved.

अभिमुखम् *ind.* Towards, facing.

अभिषिक्त *pass. part.* (*of the vb.* षिच, Sprinkle, *with* अभि, No 130.) Sprinkled, anointed, inaugurated.

अभिषेक्तुम् *inf.* To inaugurate. (*See preceding word.*)

अमी *nom. pl. m. of* अदस्, This. अमुम् *acc. sin. m.*

अयम् *nom. sin. m. of* **इदम्**, This.

अयोध्या *s. f.* Name of the capital of Ráma, *Ayodhyá*, the modern Oude.—**याम्** *loc. sin.*

अरण्यानी *nom. sin. s. f.* A large forest.

अरि *s. m.* An enemy.

अर्थम् *acc. sin. m.* A thing, wealth, meaning. *ind.* For, on account of.

अर्थवृद्धिः *nom. sin. s. f.* Tatp. Increase of wealth.

अर्थी *nom. sin. m. of* **अर्थिन्** (*from the vb.* **अर्थ**, Ask), Asking, begging. **अर्थिना** *ins. s.*

अलभमान *pres. part.* (*of the vb.* **लभ** *1st cl. átm.* Gain, *with* **अ** *priv.*) Not gaining, or getting hold of.

अलस *adj.* Lazy.

अवतारित *pass. part. of* **तारि** (*caus. of the vb.* **तॄ**, Cross, *with* **अव**), Taken off, laid down, or aside.

अवतिष्ठते *3d pers. sin. pres. of the vb.* **ष्ठा** *1st cl. átm.* (No. 38), Stand off, keep aloof.

अवदत् *3d pers. sin. 1st pret. of the vb.* **वद** *1st. cl. par.* Say.

अवधीरित *pass. part.* (*of the vb.* **अवधीर** *10th cl.*) Despised, disregarded. **अवधीर्य** *ind. pret. part.*

अवलोकयामास *3d pers. sin. 2d pret.* (No. 55, *of the vb.* **लोक** *10th cl. par.* Look, see. *with* **अव**), He looked down upon. [It is to be observed that all verbs of the 10th cl., and, among others, all derivative verbs, such as causals, &c., take a compound form of the 2d pret. In this compound tense the radical verb is combined with the 2d pret. of the auxiliary **अस**, 'to be,' **भू**, 'to become,' or **कृ**, 'to make,'—the syllable **आम्** being interposed between the radical verb and the auxiliary.] **अवलोकितः** *n. sin. m. pass. part.* Seen, beheld.

अवलोक्य *ind. pret. part.* Having seen, or looked down upon. [The indeclinable preterite, or conjunctive, participle, No. 60, ends in **य** *ya*, instead of **त्वा** *twá*, when the verb is a compound, or is preceded by a preposition.]

अवश्य, Inevitable. **अवश्यम्** *ind.* Inevitably.

अवसीदथ *2d pers. pl. pres. of the vb* **सद**, Sink, *with* **अव**, Yield, sink, give way.

अवस्थानेन *ins. sin. n.* A staying, residing.

अवस्थाप्य *ind. pret. part. of* **स्थापि** (*caus. of the vb.* **ष्ठा**, Stand, *with* **अव**), Having fixed, placed, set, or put.

अवस्थितान् *acc. pl. m.* Engaged in, prosecuting.

अवचार्य *ind. pret. part. of* **चारि** (*caus. of the vb.* **चर**, Go, *with* **वि**

and अ *priv.*) Not having deliberated, without due deliberation.

अश्रावि 3*d pers. sin.* 3*d pret. pass. of the vb.* श्रु, Hear.

अष्टाङ्गपात *s. m.* Prostration, as in reverence (—a falling on the eight members or parts of the body, viz., the hands, breast, forehead, &c.)

असमर्थः *nom. sin. m.* Unable.

असमीक्ष्य *ind. pret. part.* (*of the vb.* ईक्ष, See, *with* सम्, Completely, *and* अ *priv.*) Not having well inspected. असमीक्ष्यकारिणः *gen. sin. m.* Acting without circumspection.

असाधनाः *nom. pl. m. of* असाधन *adj.* Destitute of means, materials, or instruments.

असि 2*d pers. sin. pres. of* अस, 2*d cl. par.* Be. (No. 93.)

असौ *nom. sin. m. f. of* अदस्, He, she, that.

अस्ति 3*d p. s. pres.* (*of* अस 2*d cl. par.* Be), There is, it is. अस्तु 3*d pers. sin. imp.* Let there be, be it.

अस्मद् *crude form of the pers. pron.* I, (No. 81,) *used only in composition, implying,* My, mine, our.

अस्मिन् *loc. sin. m. or n. of* इदम्. This. अस्मै *dat. sin. m.* अस्य *gen. sin m. or n.*

अहम् *nom. sin of* अस्मद्, I. (No. 81.)

अहह *interj.* Aha!

अहो *interj.* Ah! Oh! Alas!

आ *á.*

आ *prep.* To, at, as far as, until. *When prefixed to a noun, it governs the abl. or acc. case. Prefixed to verbs denoting* Giving *and* Going, *it imparts to them the sense of* Taking *and* Coming. (No. 130).

आकर्ण्य *ind. pret. part.* (*of* कर्ण, Hear *with prep.* आ), Having heard, or listened to.

आकीर्ण *pass. part.* (*of* कॄ, Scatter, *with prep.* आ), Scattered.

आकुलः *nom. sin. m. adj.* Affected distressed.

आकुलित *pass. part.* (*of* कुल, *with* आ), Agitated, distressed.

आकृष्ट *pass. part.* (*of* कृष, Draw, *with* आ), Drawn, attracted, lured.

आखु *s. m.* A rat, or a mouse.

आगतः *nom. sin. pass. part.* (*of* गम, Go, *with* आ, No. 130), Come, arrived. आगत्य *ind. pret. part.* Having come. (See Nos. 59 and 60, and also, in the vocabulary, under the word अवलोक्य *avalokya.*)

आगम्यताम् *imp. pass.* Let there be come (by so and so).

आज्ञा *s. f.* An order, command.

आज्ञापयति *3d sin. of* **ज्ञापि** (*caus. of* **ज्ञा**, Know, *with* **आ**, No. 130), Commandeth. **यथाज्ञापयति देवः**, As your Majesty commands.

आत्मा *nom. sin. of* **आत्मन्** *m.* (No. 9), Soul, self, spirit; *acc.* **आत्मानम्**.

आदयः *nom. pl. of* **आदि** *s. m.* A beginning. In BAHUVRÍHI *compounds, it is conveniently translated by* 'et cetera,' *or*, 'and the rest'; *as* **इन्द्रादयः सुराः** The gods, INDRA, and the rest; *literally*, the gods, commencing with INDRA.

आदाय *ind. pret. part.* (*of* **दा**, Give, *with* **आ**, *which see—as also under* **अवलोक्य**), Having taken.

आदि *s. m.* A beginning. **आदि** *and also* **आदिकम्** *ind. in compos.* Et cetera, the rest. *See* **आदयः**, *above.*

आदिष्टः *nom. sin. m.* (*rt.* **दिश** *6th cl.* Show, *with* **आ**), Enjoined.

आद्यः *nom. sin. m.* First.

आधिक्यम् *nom. sin. n.* Pre-eminence.

आधिपत्यम् *nom. sin. n.* Sovereignty.

आध्मात (*rt.* **ध्मा**, Blow, *with* **आ**), Inflated.

आनीतेन *ins. sin m.* Brought, fetched. (*rt.* **णी**, Lead, *with* **आ**.)

आपदम् *acc. sin. of* **आपद्** *s. f.* Calamity.

आयान्तम् *acc. sin. m. pres part.* (*of rt.* **या** *2d cl. par.* Go, *with* **आ**,—*which see*), Coming, approaching.

आरण्य *adj.* Forest, wild, grown in the forest.

आरभ्यताम्, Let there be commenced. (See No. 132, *rt.* **रभ** *1st cl. átm.* Begin. *Usually with* **आ** *prefixed.*)

आराधितः (*rt.* **राध**, Complete, *with* **आ**), Conciliated.

आरुह्य, Having mounted. **आरूढः** *nom. sin. m. pass. part.* (No. 52, *rt.* **रुह**.)

आर्त्त, Afflicted, disturbed. (*rt.* **ऋ**.)

आर्य्य, Venerable, a friend.

आलोचितम्, (It was) considered, seen fit. **आलोच्य**, Having considered. (*rt.* **लोच**, See.)

आवाभ्याम् *inst. du.* By us two. (Nos. 81 *and* 123.)

आवृत *pass. part.* (*rt.* **वृ**, Surround), Surrounded, overspread. **आवृते**, *loc. sin. n.* (N. B. *The locative 'absolute' is analogous to the 'ablative absolute' of the Latin.*)

आशा *s. f.* Desire, hope.

आशु *ind.* Quickly, speedily.

आश्रय *s. m.* Dwelling, asylum, protection.

आसक्त *pass. part.* (*rt.* **षञ्ज**, Adhere), Attached, fixed, intent on.

आसन्न *pass. part.* (*rt.* **षद**, Go), Near, adjacent.

आस्ते *3d sin. pres.* (*rt.* **आस**, Sit, be present,—*2d cl. átm.*) He is, exists.

आस्थिताः *nom. pl.* Stayed, dwelt.

आह 3d *sin. of* आह *defective verb,* Say. *See* ब्रू.

आहार *m.* Food.

आहूय, Having called. *rt.* ह्वे. (*See* अवलोक्य.)

आहृत *pass. part.* Brought.

इ *i.*

इच्छा *f.* A desire.

इच्छन्ति, They desire. (*rt.* इष, *irreg. cf.* गच्छति, No. 38.)

इति *ind.* Thus, to this effect, so: saying. *This particle is used when the very words or thoughts of another are given, answering the purpose of the inverted comma; as* कोऽत्रेत्यहमिति ब्रूयात् (Being asked) 'Who is there?' he should say 'I.' (No. 90.)

इदम् *nom. or acc. sin. n.* This.

इह, Here, in this world.

इहसमये *loc. sin.* Here, now, at such a time as this.

ई *i.*

ईश्वर, A lord, master.

उ *u.*

उक्त *pass. part.* (*rt.* वच), Spoken. (Nos. 53 *and* 95.) उक्तवन्तौ, They two said (*indef. past. part.* No. 126.)

उक्त्वा, Having said. (No. 61.)

उच्चैस् *ind.* Up, aloud.

उड्डीयमान *pres. part.* Flying. (*rt.* डी, Fly, 4*th cl. átm., with* उत्, Up.)

उत्कर्ष *m.* Superiority, elevation.

उत्तम, Highest, best.

उत्तरदायक, Impertinent, giving (pert) answers.

उत्तरम् *nom. or acc. n.* Answer, reply.

उत्तरा *s. f.* The north. उत्तरापथ *s. n.* The north, the northern road or course.

उत्तिष्ठ, Arise, get up. (*rt.* ष्ठा, Stand.) उत्थातुम् (No. 124), To get up. उत्थापयामि, I raise. (स्थापि *caus. with* उत्, *which always requires the initial* स् *to be dropped.*) उत्थाप्य *ind. pret. part.* Having lifted, or picked up.

उत्थाय, Having arisen. (*See preceding word.*)

उत्पतितेन *ins. sin. pass. part.* (*rt.* पत, Fall, *with* उत्, Up), Springing up.

उत्पाद्य, Having raised, accumulated, (*from* पादि *caus. of* पद, Go, *with* उत्, Up).

उत्सृज्य, Having abandoned. (*rt.* सृज, Create, *with* उत्).

उदक *n.* Water.

उदकार्थी, Desirous of water.

उन्मत्त, Mad. (*rt.* मद्, Be proud.)

उपकल्पित, Prepared, made, (*from rt.* कृप, Be able).

उपक्रीय, Having bought. (*rt.* क्री, Buy.)

उपक्षय *m.* Waste, loss.

उपगच्छामि, I go near. (*rt.* गम, Go, No. 38.) उपगत *pass. part.* (No. 52.) उपगम्य *ind. pret. part.*

उपढौकयामः, We (will) make respectful offering. (*A nominal verb from* उपढौकन, A respectful offering or present.)

उपत्यका *f.* Land lying at the foot of a mountain; a valley,—कायाम् *loc. sin.*

उपदिश, Do thou advise instruct. (*rt.* दिश, 6*th cl. par.* Point out).

उपदेश *m.* Instruction, advice.

उपयोग *m.* Need of, occasion for.

उपरि *ind.* Upon, above, up, aloft, over. With.

उपविष्टौ *du. m.* The two alighted, or sat down. (*rt.* विश, Enter.)

उपशम *m.* Abatement, cessation.

उपसृत्य, Having gone near.

उपान्त *m.* edge, outskirts.

उपाय *m.* Means, resource, device.

उपार्जितानाम् *pass. part. gen. pl.* Acquired, gained. (*rt.* अर्ज, Acquire.)

उपेक्षा *f.* Neglect, disdain.

उवाच, He said, spoke to. (*rt.* वच, *cf.* No. 57.)

ऊ *ú.*

ऊचतुः, They two said. (*rt.* वच.) ऊचुः 3*d pl.* 2*d pret.* (No. 55.)

ए *e.*

एक, One, a, sole.

एकदा, One day, on a certain time.

एकैकम् *ind.* One by one.

एतद् *nom. or acc. sin. n. of* एतद् This. *acc. sin. m.* एनम्.

एव, Also, truly, selfsame.

एवम्, Thus, so.

ओ *o.*

ओषधि *s f.* An annual plant or herb.

औ *au.*

औषध *s. n.* Medicament, drug, herb or mineral.

क *ka.*

कङ्कणम् *nom. or acc. sin. s. n.* A bracelet. (No. 7.)

कच्छ *m.* The bank of a river.

कच्छप *m.* A tortoise or turtle.

कटक *m. n.* A camp, town, dwelling.

कणान् *acc. pl. of* कण *s. m.* An atom, a grain. कणैः *ins. pl.*

कथं कथमपि *ind.* Somehow or other.

कथम्, How?

कथयामि, I tell. (*rt.* कथ 10*th cl.*

par. Say, declare, relate.) कथयति 3d *pers. sin.*

कथा *f.* A story, tale, fable, narrative.

कथ्यते, It is told or declared. (No. 91.) कथ्यताम्, Let (it) be told. (No. 132.)

कदाचित् *ind.* On a certain time, at any time, ever.

कनक *m.* Gold. कनकसूत्र *s. n.* TATP. A gold-cord.

कन्दर *m. or n.* A cave, glen.

कपर्दक *m.* A small shell used as a coin, a cowrie.

कपोताः *nom. pl. of* कपोत *m.* A pigeon.

कम्पमानान् *acc. pl. of pres. part. of* कप (इ) 1*st cl. átm.* To tremble, shake.

करटक *m.* The name of a certain jackal.

करणीय, To be made or done. (*fut. part. pass.*, No. 127, *of* कृ. *See* No. 101.)

कराला, Name of a certain woman.

करिष्यथ, You will do. (2*d fut.*, Nos. 28 *and* 118, *of* कृ, No. 101.)

कर्त्तरिका *f.* A knife, or couteau de chasse.

कर्त्तव्यताम् *acc. sin. abs. s. f.* Suitable measures. (No. 127.)

कर्पूर *m. or n.* Camphor.

कलश *m.* An earthern jar.

कलहेन *ins. sin. of* कलह *m.* Contention, strife.

कलिङ्ग, Name of a district on the *Coromandel* coast, extending from below *Cuttak* to the vicinity of *Madras.*

कस्मिंश्चित् *loc. sin. m. of* किञ्चित्, *pron.* A certain. (Nos. 86 *and* 81.)

काकैः *ins. pl. of* काक *m.* A crow.

काककूर्ममृगाखुवत् *ind.* Like the crow, tortoise, deer, and mouse. (काक कूर्म मृग आखु वत्, *see* Nos. 104 *and* 73.)

काककूर्मादीनाम्, Of the crow, and the tortoise, and the rest. (*gen. pl. m., see last word, and also under* आदयः.)

काकी *f.* A hen-crow.

काय *m.* The body. कायक्लेश *m.* TATP. Pain of body.

कारयित्वा, Having caused to be made or done. (*ind. pret. part. of* कारि *caus. of* कृ, No. 101.) कारित *pass. part.* (No. 52.)

कारिन् *agt.* Making, a maker.—णः *nom. pl. m. or gen. sin.*

कार्य्य *fut. pass. part.* Proper to be made or done. *See* करणीय.

काल *m.* Time. A name of the destroying deity.

काव्य *n.* Poetry, a poem.

काश्मीर *n.* Cashmere.

किञ्चित् *nom. or acc. n.* Some, any thing. (No. 86.) *ind.* Somewhat.

किम् *nom. or acc. sin. n.* Who? which? what? *ind.* why? what! whether. (No. 85. Obs. *It is often employed with the force merely of a note of interrogation*). *When* **अपि** *is subjoined, it gives an indeterminate sense,—thus,* **किमपि**, Somewhat, some, any, any thing soever.

किमर्थम् *ind.* On what account?

किमिति *ind.* How so? What's this?

किम्वदन्ती *s. f.* Rumour, on dit.

कियत् *adj.* Some, a little. How long?

कुक्कुर *m.* A dog.

कुतस् *ind.* Whence? wherefore? **कुत्रोऽपि**, Somewhere or other. (*See under* **किम्**.)

कुतूहल *n.* Eagerness, joy, curiosity.

कुपित, Angry. (*pass. part. of* **कुप**.)

कुम्भ *m.* A jar **कुम्भकार** *m.* A potter.

कुरुत 2d *pl. imp. of* **कृ**, Do, make. **कुर्वाण** *pres. part. átm*

कुश *m.* A species of grass used in many religious observances, hence called sacrificial grass. (Poa cynosuroides.) **कुशहस्त**, BAHUV. With *Kuśa* grass in hand.

कुशल *n.* Health, welfare.

कूप *m.* A well.

कूर्म *m.* A tortoise.

कृत, Made, done. (*pass. part.* No. 52, *of* **कृ**, No. 101.)

कृतवान्, He made. (No. 126.)

कृते *ind.* For, on account of.

कृष्ण *adj.* Black, or dark blue. **कृष्णसर्प**, A black snake. (No. 69.)

केनचित्, By some one. (*ins. sin. of* **किञ्चित्**, *q. v.*)

केनापि, By some one. (*ins. sin. of* **किमपि**, *q. v.*)

केशर *m.* A lion's mane.

कोटर *m. n.* The hollow of a tree.

कोदण्ड *m. n.* A bow.

कोप *m.* Anger.

क्रम *m.* Course, order, way.

क्रोड *n.* The bosom, a cavity.

क्लेश *m.* Pain, distress.

क्व, Where? whither?

क्षणात्, Instantly. (*from* **क्षण** *m.* A moment,—*the abl. being used adverbially*).

क्षत्रिय *m.* A soldier.

क्षन्तव्य, To be suffered, endured patiently. (*fut. pass. part.*, No. 127, *of* **क्षम**.)

क्षीणपाप, BAHUV. Purified—(his sins being wiped out when he has suffered the consequences of them).

क्षुधा *f.* Hunger.

क्षौर *m.* A shaving (of the head). **क्षौरकरण** *n.* The operation of shaving.

ख *kha.*

खण्डित, Broken, shivered. (*rt.* **खड इ**).

खादामि, I eat. (*rt.* खाद् 1*st. cl. par.*) —खादित, *pass. part.*

खुर *m.* A hoof. खुरत्रये, On three legs.

ग *ga.*

गच्छ, Go thou. (No. 38.) गच्छत्सु *loc. pl. n. pres. part.* (No. 125. *See also under* आवृत.)

गणेशाय, To GANEŚA, the deity of wisdom.

गत, Gone, went. (No. 53.)

गमिष्यामि, I will go. (Nos. 28, 118, *and* 121, *rt.* गम.)

गम्भीर, Deep.

गर्द्दभ *m.* An ass.

गर्भ *m.* The interior, or middle.

गल *m.* The throat.

गृध्र *m.* A vulture. गृध्रचक्राभ्यां *ins. du.* DWAN. By the vulture and the crane.

गृह *n.* A house, home. गृहरक्षा TATP. The guarding of a house.

गृहीत *pass. part. of* ग्रह, Take. (Nos. 102 *and* 53.) गृह्यताम्, Let be taken, or accepted. (No. 132.)

गोदावरी *f.* The (river) *Godávarí.*

गौरव *n.* Respectability, weight, importance, respect.

ग्रहीष्यति, He will collect. (*rt.* ग्रह; *see under* गृहीत.)

ग्राम *m.* A village. (*In composition,* A multitude.)

ग्रीवा *f.* The neck, throat.

घ *gha.*

घट *m.* An earthen water-jar

घण्टा *f.* A bell.

घण्टाकर्ण *s. m.* (Bell-ear) Name of a supposed demon.

घन *m. n.* A cloud. घनगर्जित *n.* TATP. The roar of a (thunder) cloud.

च *cha.*

च *ind.* And.

चकित, Alarmed. (*rt.* चक.)

चक्र *m.* The ruddy or Brahmany goose (anas casarca).

चञ्च्वा *ins. sin. of* चञ्चु *f.* A bird's beak or bill. चञ्चुभिः *ins. pl.*

चतुष्टय *n.* The aggregate of four, a quarternion.

चन्द्रभागा *f.* The *Chinnáb* (river in the *Punjaub*).

चन्द्रार्द्धचूडामणि *m.* Whose crest-jewel is the half-moon (a name of the god ŚIVA).

चरण *m.* The foot.

चरन् *nom. sin. m. of* चरत् *pres. part.*, No. 125, *of* चर 1*st cl. par.* Go, *also* feed, graze.

चलति, Moves, goes. (*rt.* चल.) *pass. part.* चलित, Moved, went.

चित्कार *m.* A scream, a bray.

चित्र *adj.* Variegated, wonderful, lovely. चित्राङ्ग *m.* Spotted or streaked in the body.

चिन्तयति, He thinks, reflects. (*rt.* चित इ 10*th cl. par.*) —यन्ति 3*d pl.* चिन्तित *pass. part.* चिन्तनीय *fut. pass. part.*

चिन्ता *f.* Thought, care.

चिरकालपालित, Cherished for a long time. TATP. (*rt.* पाल 10*th cl. par.*)

चूडा *f.* Top, summit, crest. चूडामणि *m.* TATP. A jewel in a crest or diadem.

चूर्णित, Smashed to pieces. (*rt.* चूर्ण).

चेत् *ind.* If. Although.

चेष्टा *f.* Any bodily motion or gesture. Action. चेष्टानिरूपण *n.* TATP. The observing of a person's actions.

चौर *m.* A thief.

छ *chha.*

छिनत्ति, He cuts. (*rt.* छिद 7*th cl. par.*) छिन्न *pass. part.* छिन्नद्रुम *m.* KARM. A riven tree. छिन्नबन्धन BAHUV. Whose bonds were cut. छेत्स्यामि, I will cut.

ज *ja.*

जन, A person. जनप्रवाद *m.* TATP. Rumour, report.

जम्बुक, A jackal.

जल *n.* Water. जलधर, *m.* A cloud (water-holder). जलाशय *m.* A lake. जलाशयान्तरम् *nom. or acc. sin. n.* Another lake. जलाश्रय *m.* A lake.

जागर्त्ति, He awakes. (*rt.* जागृ 2*d cl. par.*) जागरयसि *caus.* Thou dost waken.

जात *pass. part.* Born. (*rt.* जन, Be born.) जातविश्वास BAHUV. Having his confidence excited. जातामर्ष BAHUV. Having one's anger roused.

जालम् *nom. or acc. sin. n.* A net.

जीवित *n.* Life. जीविताशा *f.* TATP. Hope of life.

ज्ञाति, A kinsman. ज्ञातयः *nom. pl.*

त *ta.*

तच्छ्रुत्वा, Having heard that. (*See* No. 112.)

तण्डुल *m.* Rice. तण्डुलकण *m.* TATP. A grain of rice.

तत् *ind.* Therefore, so. Then.

ततस् *ind.* (*equivalent to* तस्मात्, No. 81.) Thence, from that. Afterwards. ततः प्रभृति *ind.* Thenceforward.

तत्क्षणात् *ind.* Instantly.

तत्र *ind.* There.

तथा, So. तथाविध *adj.* Of such a sort, or in such a plight.

तदनुसरणक्रमेण *ins. n.* TATP. By the way, or in the course, of following him.

तन्मध्यात् *abl. sin.* TATP. From amongst them.

तम्, Him. (No. 81.)

तरुः *nom. sin. m.* A tree. तरोः *gen.* तरौ *loc.* तरून् *acc. pl.* तरुषु *loc. pl.* तरुतल *n.* TATP. The foot of a tree.

तर्हि *conj.* Then.

तल *n.* The lower part, bottom, foot.

तस्मिन् *loc. sin. m. or n.* (*of* तद्, No. 81.) He, she, it, that. तस्यै *dat. sin. f.* तस्याः *abl. or gen. sin. f.*

ताडयामास 3*d sin.* 2*d pret. of* तड, 10*th cl. par.* Beat, castigate. ताडयित्वा *ind. pret. part.* ताडित *pass. part.*

तावत् *ind.* So far, so much. Just, at least.

तिलक *m.* A sectarial mark (made on the forehead with coloured earths).

तिष्ठति, He stands. (*rt.* स्था 1*st cl. par. See* No. 38.)

तीर *n.* A shore, a bank. तीरे *loc.*

तु *ind.* But.

तुल्यविक्रमे *loc. sin. m.* BAHUV. Of equal prowess.

तुष्ट *pass. part.* Pleased. (*rt.* तुष 4*th cl. par.*)

तूष्णीम् *ind.* Silently, softly.

तृण *n.* Grass.

ते, They. (*See* तद्, No. 81.) *Also dat. or gen. sin. of* युष्मद्, Thou.

तेन, By him, or that.

त्यज्यताम् 3*d sin. imp. pass.* (No. 132) *of* त्यज 1*st cl. par.* Abandon.

त्रय *n. in compos.* A set of three; *as,* भुवनत्रय, The three worlds, *i.e.,* Heaven, Earth, and Hell.

त्रास *m.* Fear, fright. त्रासित, Frightened. *pass. part. of* त्रासि *caus. of vb.* त्रस, Fear.

त्वम्, Thou. (*See* No. 81.)

द *da.*

दक्षिण *adj.* Southern. दक्षिणा *s.f.* The south. दक्षिणापथ *n.* The southern road or course.

दत्त्वा, Having given. (3*d cl. par. rt.* दा; *see* No. 61.)

दधि *n.* Curds. दधिकर्ण *m.* Curd-ear (name of a certain cat).

दमनक, Name of a certain jackal.

दम्पती *nom. du. m.* DWANDWA, Wife and husband, a wedded pair.

दर्प *m.* Pride.

दर्पण *m.* A mirror.

दर्शन *n.* Sight, vision.

दर्शय 2*d sin. imp. of* दर्शि *caus. of* दृश. See (No. 38) दर्शयतु 3*d sin. imp.* दर्शयन् *nom. sin. pres. part.* (No. 125.) दर्शित *pass. part.* दर्शितवान् *nom. sin. m. indef. pass. part.* (No. 126). दर्शयित्वा *ind. pret. part.*

दान *n.* A gift. Liberality.

दारिद्र्य *n.* Poverty.

दिग्देशात् Dwandwa. From quarters and countries (*comp.* दिश् + देश).

दिग्विजय *m.* Tatp. The subjugation of a country.

दीर्घ *adj.* Long. *ind. n.* Deeply. **दीर्घराव** Bahuv. Making a long-continued noise, yelling, howling.

दुरात्मन् *adj.* Bad-souled, vile.

दुर्ग *adj.* Difficult of access; *s. n.* A fort.

दुर्दान्त *pass. part. of* दम, To tame (*with* दुर् *prep.* Difficult), Hard to be tamed.

दुष्ट, Corrupt, bad.

दूर *adj.* Far, distant. **दूरीकृत**, Put to a distance.

दृषद् *f.* A stone or rock.

दृष्ट *pass. part. of* दृश, See. **दृष्ट्वा** Having seen.

दृष्टि *f.* The eye. Sight, a look. **दृष्टिप्रसाद** *m.* The favour of a look.

देव, A god. A king (*in poetical language*). **देवीकोट्ट** *m.* The city of *Vána* on the Coromandel coast.

देह *n.* The body.

दोष *m.* A fault, defect, evil.

द्रव्य *n.* A thing, substance: property, wares, goods, chattels.

द्रुतम् *ind.* Swiftly.

द्वन्द्व *n.* Strife.

द्वार् *f.* A door. **द्वारि** *loc. sin.*

ध *dha.*

धनुषि *loc. sin. of* धनुष् *n.* A bow.

धन्य, Happy, fortunate.

धरिष्यति, He will place. (*rt.* धृ.)

धारा *f.* The sharp edge (of a sword or the like). **धारासार** *m.* Tatp. A heavy fall of rain.

धावताम् *gen. pl. of* धावत् *pres. part.* (No. 125) *of* धाव 1*st cl. par.* Run.

धीमताम् *gen. pl. m. of* धीमत्, Wise.

धृत *pass. part. of* धृ, Hold, seize, place.

न *na.*

न *ind.* No, not.

नः *acc. dat. or gen. pl. of* अस्मद्, I.

नकुल *m.* An ichneumon or mungoose.

नगर *n.* A city. **नगरे** *loc.*

नदी *f.* A river.

ननाद 3*d sin.* 2*d pret. of* नद, Bellow, roar.

नभस् *n.* The sky. **नभस्तल** *n.* Tatp. The nether sky, the atmosphere.

नरपति Tatp. A lord of men, a king.

नर्दित *pass. part. of* नर्द, Roar, bellow. *s. n.* A roar.

नश्यति, He perishes. (*rt.* नश 4*th cl. par.*)

नाना *ind.* Many, various, sundry.

नाम *nom. or acc. sin. of* नामन् *n.*

A name (No. 9). *ind.* By name, indeed. *Often an emphatic particle.*

नामन् *n.* A name. *This word most usually occurs as the last member of a Bahuvríhi or adjectival compound* (No. 107).

नामा *nom. sin. m.* नामानम् *acc.*

नाम्नि *loc.*

निःस्वादु *adj.* Tasteless.

निक्षिप्य, Having thrown in. (*rt.* क्षिप *6th cl. par.* Throw.)

निद्रा *f.* Sleep. निद्रया *ins.*

निधाय, Having placed, deposited. (*rt.* धा, Hold.)

निपतित *pass. part.* Fallen down or in. (*rt.* पत *1st cl. par.* Fall.) निपातित *caus.* Made to fall. Killed.

निभृत, Secret. निभृतम् *ind.* Privately.

निमग्न *pass. part.* Immersed. (*rt.* मस्ज *6th cl. par.*)

नियोज्य, Having yoked. (*rt.* युज *10th cl. par.*)

निराश *adj.* Without hope, hopeless.

निरूपित *pass. part.* Investigated. Narrated. (*rt.* रूप *10th cl. par.*) निरूप्यताम् *3d sin. imp. pass.* निरूप्यमाण *pres. part. pass.* Being discovered.

निर्जन *adj.* Lonely (निर्, Without, *and* जन, People).

निर्दयम् *ind.* Unmercifully.

निर्बुद्धि *adj.* Senseless. निर्बुद्धेः *gen. sin.*

निर्भरम् *ind.* Excessively.

निर्मित *pass. part.* Meted out, constructed. (*rt.* मा, Measure.)

निर्वात *adj.* Free from wind, sheltered. *s. m.* A calm.

निर्विशेष *adj.* Same, like, having no difference.

निर्वृत *adj.* Happy, at ease.

निवसति, He dwells in. (*rt.* वस, Dwell.) निवसन्ति *3d pl.*

निवेदितम् *nom. sin. n.* Word was brought or sent. (*rt.* विद्, Know. वेदि *caus.*)

निश्चेष्ट, Motionless.

निहत *pass. part.* Smitten, slain. (*rt.* हन, Slay.) निहतसेनयोः *gen. du. m.* Bahuv. Having their armies slain, or greatly cut up.

नीड *m.* A nest.

नीत्वा, Having conducted. Having passed (a space of time). (*rt.* णी, Lead.)

नील *adj.* Black, or dark blue. *s. n.* Indigo (the dye). नीलवर्ण Bahuv. Blue-coloured. नीली *f.* The indigo-plant.

नूनम् *ind.* Assuredly.

नृपति, A king.

प *pa.*

पक्षिणः *nom. pl. of.* पक्षिन्, A bird. पक्षिभिः *ins. pl.*

पङ्क *m.* Mire, a slough. **पङ्के** *loc.*

पञ्चत्वम् *acc. sin. of* **पञ्चत्व** *abs s. n.* (*from* **पञ्चन्**, Five), Death (*i.e.* reduction to the state of the five separate elements, of whose aggregate the body consists).

पट *m. n.* Cloth, a web.

पटल *n.* A heap or multitude. A coating or covering.—**लैः** *ins. pl.*

पतित *pass. part. of* **पत**, Fall.

पत्नी *f.* A wife. **पत्न्या** *ins.*

पथिन् *m.* A road. **पथि** *loc.*

पद *n.* The foot. Place, station. A degree, step. Post, rank.

पन्थानः *nom. pl. of* **पथिन्**, A road or path.

पपात 3*d sin.* 2*d pret. of* **पत**, Fall.

पर *pronominal,* Other. Extreme, pre-eminent.

पराक्रम *m.* Power, valour. Forcible means.

परिचीयते 3*d sin. pres. pass.* (No. 91), Is known or found out. (*rt.* **चि**, Collect.)

परिजन *m.* Followers, retinue.

परित्यक्त *pass. part.* Quitted, abandoned. **परित्यज्य** *ind. pret. part.* (*rt.* **त्यज**, Quit.)

परिदेवन *n.* Complaint, lamentation.

परिभूत, Despised.

परिभ्रमन्, Prowling, roaming. (No. 125, *rt.* **भ्रम** 1*st cl. par.* Whirl.)

परिवार *m.* Retinue.

परिवृत *pass. part.* Surrounded, attended. (*rt.* **वृ**, Surround.)

परिश्रान्त *pass. part.* Wearied. (*rt.* **श्रम**, Be weary.)

पर्यटता *ins. sin. m. of* **पर्यटत्**, *pres. part.* Prowling about. (*rt.* **अट**, Travel.)

पलायमान *pres. part.* Fleeing. (*rt.* **अय**, 1*st cl. átm.* Go, *with* **परा**, Back, *the* **र्** *being changed to* **ल्**.) **पलायित** *pass. part.*

पशु *m.* A beast. **पशून्** *acc. pl.* **पशुभिः** *ins. pl.* **पशूनाम्** *gen. pl.*

पश्चात् *ind.* After, afterwards. Behind.

पश्यामि, I see. (*rt.* **दृश**, No. 38.) **पश्य** 2*d sin. imp.* Behold.

पाटलिपुत्रनामधेय BAHUV. Named Páṭaliputra (*a city, see* No. 107, *supposed to be the ancient Palibothra and the modern Patna*).

पाणि *m.* The hand.

पातित *pass. part. of* **पाति** (*caus. of* **पत**, Fall), Made to fall, thrown down.

पाद *m.* A foot.

पानीय *n.* Water (*fut. part. pass. of* **पा**, Drink, No. 127).

पान्थ, O traveller! **पान्थेन** *ins.*

पापीयान्, More, or very, wicked. (*compar. of* **पाप**, Wicked).

पार्वण *m.* The general funeral ceremony, with double oblations to the manes, at the *Parva*, or conjunction of the sun and moon.

पाश *m.* A snare, fetter. पाशहस्त BAHUV. Snare-in-hand.

पिङ्गल *adj.* Tawny, yellowish; *hence* पिङ्गलक, the name of a certain lion.

पिपासा *f.* Thirst, a desire to drink.

पीडित *pass. part.* Pressed, pained, distressed. (*rt.* पीड 10*th cl. par.* To give pain.)

पीत्वा, Having drunk. (*rt.* पी or पा.)

पुच्छ *m.* A tail. पुच्छाग्र *n.* TATP. The tip of the tail.

पुनर् *and before certain letters* पुनः *ind.* Again. Assuredly.

पुर् *f.* A city. पुरि *loc. sin.*

पुरस्तात् *ind.* Before, in front.

पूग *m.* Betel-nut.

पूज्य, Worshipped, deserving adoration. (*fut. pass. part. of* पूज 10*th cl. átm.*)

पूर्ण, Filled. (*pass. part. of* पूर, Fill.)

पूर्व्वक *adj.* Prior, before, preceding. *This word frequently forms the last member in a compound; as* अननुभूतपूर्व्वक, Never previously perceived.

पृच्छति, He asks. (*rt.* प्रच्छ 6*th cl. par.*)

पृष्ठ *n.* The back. The surface. The flat roof of a house. पृष्ठे *loc. sin.*

प्रक्षिप्त, Flung, cast. (*rt.* क्षिप 6*th par.*)

प्रचलित *pass. part.* Moved forwards, departed, went. (*rt.* चल, Go).

प्रच्छन्न *pass. part.* Covered, concealed. (*rt.* छद 1*st or* 10*th cl. par.* To cover.)

प्रणम्य, Having made obeisance. (*rt.* णम 1*st cl. par.* Bow.)

प्रति *prep.* Again, against, back again. *As a postposition it governs the accusative case, and then means,* Towards, to, with, in regard to.

प्रतिक्षणम् *ind.* Every moment, continually.

प्रतिज्ञा *f.* A promise. प्रतिज्ञात, Promised, propounded. (*rt.* ज्ञा, Know.)

प्रतिबिम्ब *n.* A reflected image.

प्रत्यहम् *ind.* Daily, every day.

प्रत्यावृत्य, Having returned. (*rt.* वृत, Be, *with* आ *and* प्रति.)

प्रथम *adj.* First.

प्रभाव *m.* Power.

प्रभूत *adj.* Much, abundant.

प्रभृति *ind. Following a noun frequently in the ablative case,* From, forward, commencing at.

प्रयत्न *m.* Effort, exertion, pains.

प्रयात *pass. part.* Set out, departed. (*rt.* या 2*d cl. par.* Go.)

प्रयोजन *n.* Cause, occasion, need, use, call for.

प्रलय *m.* Dissolution (of the world at the end of one of the periods termed a *Kalpa*).

प्रविशति, He enters. (*rt.* विश 6*th cl. par.*) प्रविष्ट *pass. part.*

प्रवृत्त *pass. part.* Going on, begun. Ensued. Engaged, occupied, busy. (*rt.* **वृत**, Be.)

प्रवेशित *pass. part. of* **वेशि** (*caus. of* **विश**, Enter), Made to enter.

प्रसाद *m.* Favour, kindness, brightness.

प्रसुप्त *pass. part.* Asleep, slept. (*rt.* **स्वप**).

प्रस्तर *m.* A stone, rock.—**रे** *loc.*

प्रस्ताव *m.* An occasional or introductory eulogium. The subject of conversation. An occasion, opportunity, season.

प्रस्तूयते, Is praised, or declared. (*rt.* **स्तु** 2*d cl. par.*)

प्रस्थापित, Dismissed, sent away. *pass. part. of* **स्थापि** *caus of* **स्था**, Stand, *with* **प्र**.

प्रहार *m.* A stroke, blow.

प्रहृष्टमनाः *nom. sin. m.* Bahuv. (*comp. of* **प्रहृष्ट**, Rejoiced, *and* **मनस्** *n.* The mind), Delighted at heart.

प्राङ्गण *n.* A court, a yard.

प्रातर् *and before certain hard consonants* **प्रातः** *ind.* Early, betimes in the morning.

प्राप्त *pass. part.* Obtained, caught, met with, found. (*rt.* **आप**, Obtain.) **प्राप्तकाल** Karm. A proper time, a fitting season.

प्रासाद *m.* A palace.

प्रिय *adj.* Beloved, dear, liked, agreeable.

ब *ba.*

बद्ध, Bound, tied, *pass. part. of* **बन्ध** 9*th cl. par.* Bind. **बद्ध्वा** *ind. pret. part.*

बध *m.* Slaughter.

बन्धन *n.* A binding, bondage. A bond, a cord.

बभूव, He became (No. 57).

बल *n.* Strength, force. An army. **बलवत्** *ind.* Stoutly, lustily. **बलवान्** *adj. nom. sin. m.* Strong. **बलात्** *adv.* Forcibly.

बहु *adj.* Much, many. Greatly.

बाणिज, *m.* A merchant. **बाणिज्य** *n.* Trade.

बाल *or* **बालक** *m.* A child. *adj.* Young. **बालापत्य** Karm. *n.* Young offspring.

बुद्धि *f.* Intellect, understanding. **बुद्धिमत्**, Intelligent. **बुद्धिमन्तः** *nom. pl. m.*

बुद्ध्वा *ind. pret. part.* (*of* **बुध**), Having supposed, or understood.

बुभुक्षा *f.* Hunger, a desire to eat.—**याम्** *loc. sin.*

ब्रह्मपुराख्य *n.* Bahuv. Named *Brahmapura* (a city).

ब्रह्मारण्य *n.* A forest of *Brahma.*

ब्रूहि, Say thou. *imp. of* **ब्रू** 2*d cl. par.* **ब्रूते**, He says, 3*d sin. pres. átm.**

* The tense-endings exhibited under No. 118 are termed by Indian grammarians, *parasmai-pada, i.e.* 'an expression for the sake of another,'—because the effect of the action

भ *bha.*

भक्षयित्वा, Having devoured. (*rt.* **भक्ष** 10*th cl. par.*) **भक्षित** *pass. part.*

भगवत् *adj.* Adorable, respectable. —**वती** *fem.*—**वत्या** *ins. sin. f.*

भग्न *pass. part of* **भञ्ज**, Break, demolish.

भद्र *adj. voc.* O worthy (Sir)!

भय *n.* Fear, alarm. **भयहेतु** TATP. *m.* A cause of alarm.

भर *m.* Burden, weight. **भरं कुर्वन्**, Resting (*lit.* making) his weight.

भवत् (*a form of address more respectful than* **त्वम्**, Thou), Your highness, worship. **भवान्** *nom. sin. m.* **भवद्भिः** *ins. pl.* **भवताम्** *gen. pl.*

भवेत् (No. 133), He should be. **भवितव्य** *fut. part. pass.* To be become.

भागीरथी *f.* The river Ganges (—so named after a pious king, *Bhagíratha*, whose austerities brought this sacred stream from heaven.

भाग्य *n.* Good fortune. **भाग्येन** *ins.*

भाण्ड *n.* Any vessel, pot, &c. A vat.

भार्या *f.* A wife.

भिक्षुक *m.* A beggar.

भुज *m.* The arm. **भुजान्तरम्** *ind.* Within the arms or embrace.

भूत्वा, Having become (No. 61).

भूमि *f.* The earth, ground, territory. **भूमौ** *loc. sin.*

भृत्य *m.* A servant. Minister.

भेतव्य *fut. pass. part. of* **भी**, Fear.

भेद *m.* A breaking, separation.

भेदयितुम् *inf. of* **भेदि** *caus. of* **भिद्**, Break, *in the sense of the simple verb,—to be rendered passively by reason of* **शक्यः**.

is supposed to pass on *parasmai* 'to another'. These, therefore, are the normal tense-endings of an active transitive verb. The tense-endings mentioned under No. 91 as being employed in the conjugation of the passive voice, are named *átmane-pada*, *i.e.* 'an expression for the sake of one's self,' because (—as in the Greek 'middle voice'—) the employment of such a tense-ending (not in the passive) supposes the action to revert *átmane*, 'to one's self'.

The *átmane-pada* tense-endings, as given by PÁṆINI, are

	Sing.	*Dual.*	*Plural.*
Lowest	त *ta*	आतां *átán*	झ *jha.*
Middle	थास् *thás*	आथां *áthán*	ध्वं *dhwam.*
Highest	इट् *iṭ*	वहि *vahi*	महिङ् *mahing.*

Altered to suit the First Conjugation, in the present, these tense-endings become

ते *te*	आते *áte*	अन्ते *ante.*
से *se*	आथे *áthe*	ध्वे *dhwe.*
ए *e*	वहे *vahe*	महे *mahe.*

भैरव *adj.* Formidable.

भोजन *n.* Food. The act of eating. (*rt.* भुज.) भोज्य *fut. part. pass.* To be eaten. *s. n.* Food; store of provisions.

भो भोस् *interj.* Ho! hark ye!

भोस् *ind. A vocative particle of respect,* Ho!

म *ma.*

मण्डपिका *f.* A shed.—कायाम् *loc.*

मण्डल *m.* or *n.* A ring, a circle.

मति *f.* The mind. Opinion, resolution.

मद *m.* Pride. Joy. Desire.

मध्य *n.* The middle, midst.

मन्त्र *m.* A mystical verse, a spell. Secret consultation, counsel. मन्त्रिन् *m.* A counsellor. मन्त्री *nom. sin.*

मन्थर *adj.* Slow. मन्थराभिधान *m.* BAHUV. Named Manthara ("the slow").

मन्द *adj.* Slow, dull, bad. मन्दं मन्दम् *ind.* Slowly slowly. मन्दादर BAHUV. Slack in (showing) respect.

मन्दिर *m.* A house, temple, town.

मन्ये, I think, suppose. (*rt.* मन 4*th cl. átm.*) मन्यन्ते 3*d pl.*

मयूर *m.* A peacock.

मरण *n.* Dying, death.

मर्कट *m.* A monkey.

मर्म्मज्ञ *agt.* Heart-knowing, wise. (*See next word.*)

मर्म्मन् *n.* Any vital organ; the heart. Secret meaning or purpose.

महत् *adj.* Great. महती *f.* महा (No. 70) *is the form which this adjective assumes as the first member of a* KARM. *or* BAHUV. *compound; as,* महापण्डित, A great *Pandit*; महास्नेह, Of great fondness; महापङ्क *m.* A great quagmire; महान् *nom. sin. m.*

मांस *n.* Flesh.

मान *m.* Rank, honour, pride. मानध्मात TATP. Puffed up with pride.

मार्ज्जार *m.* A cat.

मास *m.* A month.

मित्र *n.* A friend. मित्रलाभ *m.* TATP. The acquisition of friends.

मिलित *pass. part. of* मिल 6*th cl. par.* Meet, unite. मिलित्वा, Having assembled.

मुक्त *pass. part. of* मुच 6*th cl. par.* Release, discharge. मुक्तापद् BAHUV. Rescued from misfortune. मोचयितुम् *inf. caus.*

मुख *n.* The face, mouth.

मूर्ख *m.* A fool.

मूषिक *m.* A mouse or rat.

मृग *m.* A deer, a wild animal. मृगव्याधशूकरान् *acc. pl. m.* DWAND. The deer, the hunter, and the boar.

मृत *pass. part. of* मृ 6*th cl. átm.* Die. मृतवत् *ind.* Like one dead. मृत्यु *m.* Death.

म्रियेत 3d *sin. pot. of the preceding verb.*

य *ya.*

यक्ष *m.* A demigod, attendant chiefly on KUVERA, the god of wealth, and employed in the care of his gardens and treasures. यक्षेश्वर *m.* KUVERA (the lord of the *Yakshas*).

यत् *ind.* Because, since. That, to the following effect, saying.

यत्न *m.* Effort, exertion, pains.

यथा *ind.* As. So as. How. यथाकार्य्यम् *ind.* As is proper to act. यथा-सुखम् *ind.* Happily.

यदि *ind.* If.

यमुना *f.* The river *Yamuná* (or Jumna).

यस्य *gen. sin. m. or. n. of* यद् *rel. pron.* Who, which (*cf.* No. 81).

यातु 3d *sin. imp.* (*of* या 2d *cl. par.* Go), Let it pass. Go to.

यावत् *ind.* As soon as, as long as. यावज्जीवम् *ind.* For the rest of life.

युक्त *pass. part.* (*of* युज 7*th cl. par.* Join, *and* 4*th cl. átm.* Be suitable), Associated, possessing. Right, fit, proper.

र *ra.*

रक्त *n.* Blood.

रक्षक *m.* A guardian, protector.

रक्षा *f.* Protection.

रजक *m.* A washerman.

रस *m.* Flavour, taste. Sentiment.

राक्षस *m.* A demon, or giant.

राज *is written for* राजन् *at the end of a compound word, as, nom. sin.* महाराजः, A great king.

राजपुत्र *m.* TATP. A king's son, a prince. A man of the military tribe, a rajpoot. राजपुरुष *m.* A king's man or servant; an executive functionary.

राजा *nom. sin. of* राजन्, A king (No. 9). राज्ञा *ins.*

राज्य *n.* Sovereignty. Realm.

राव *m.* A noise. A yell.

रूप *n.* Beauty. Form. रूपयौवनवत् (—fem. —वती), Endued with beauty and youth.

रोचते, Pleases, is agreeable or liked. (*rt.* रुच 1*st cl. átm.*)

रौद्र *m.* Heat.

ल *la.*

लक्ष *n.* One hundred thousand (a lac).

लगुड *m.* A club or bludgeon.

लग्न *n.* (*In popular acceptation*) the moment of the sun's entrance into a zodiacal sign. लग्नवेला *f.* TATP. An auspicious moment.

लघुपतनकनामा *nom. sin. m.* BAHUV.

By name *Laghupatanaka* (—*i.e.* who falls, or alights, lightly).

लज्जमान *pres. part. átm. of* लस्ज 6*th cl. átm.* Be ashamed, blush.

लब्ध्वा *ind. pret. part. of* लभ 1*st. cl. átm.* Gain, obtain.

लिखतु *imp.* Let him write or scratch. (*rt.* लिख 6*th cl. par.*)

लुब्ध, Covetous, greedy. लुब्धक *m.* A hunter.

लुलोठ 3*d sin.* 2*d pret. of* लुठ, Roll, wallow.

लून *pass. part. of* लू, Cut.

लोक *m.* The world, mankind, people.

लोभ *m.* Covetousness, greediness. लोभाकृष्ट TATP. Drawn by greediness.

व *va.*

वचन *n.* A word, speech. Proposal.

वञ्चक *m.* a cheat, a jackal.

वञ्चित *pass. part.* (*of* वञ्च), Deceived.

वट *m.* The Banian, or large *Indian fig-tree* (Ficus Indica).

वत् *an indeclinable affix,* As, like.

वदामि, I say. *rt.* वद 1*st cl. par.*

वन *n.* A forest. वनदेवता *f.* TATP. A forest-deity. —तया *ins.* वनवासिन् *agt.* Forest-residing—सिभिः *ins. pl.*

वर्त्मन् *n.* A road. वर्त्मना *ins.*

वर्द्धमान *pres. part. átm.* (*of* वृद्ध 1*st cl.*), Increasing, thriving.

वर्ष *m.* A year. *m.* or *n.* Rain. वर्षाः *f. pl.* The rains, or rainy season. वर्षासु *loc.*

वस्त्र *n.* Clothes.

वहिर् *and before certain consonants* वहिः *ind.* out, outside, externally.

वा *ind.* Or, either.

वाच् *f.* Speech. वाचा *ins.*

वादयन्ति, They make to sound. *caus. of* वद, Say.

वानर *m.* A monkey.

वायस *m.* A crow. वायसी *fem.*

वारं वारम् *ind.* From time to time, ever and anon.

वास *m.* An abode.

वासर *m.* A time, turn.

वासिन् An inhabitant.

विकीर्ण *pass. part. of* कॄ, Scatter (*with* वि, *a preposition implying* Disunion, &c., No. 130, *and corresponding to the English adjuncts,* a, ex, dis, in, un, &c.). विकीर्य *ind. pret. part.*

विक्रम *m.* Valour.

विक्रीय, Having bought. *rt.* क्री 9*th cl.* Buy.

विग्रह *m.* War, strife. विग्रहयितुम्, To wage war. (*rt.* ग्रह 10*th cl.*) Take, seize.

विचित्र *adj.* Various, variegated, charming.

विज्ञप्त *or* विज्ञापित, Apprized, informed (*rt.* ज्ञा, Know; *caus.* ज्ञपि or ज्ञापि)

विज्ञाय, Having known, perceived, recognized. (*rt.* **ज्ञा**, Know.)

वित्त *n.* Wealth. **वित्तहीन** TATP. Destitute of wealth.

विदधान *pres. part. átm.* Making. (*rt.* **धा** *3d cl. par.* Hold.)

विध *m.* A mode, manner, sort.

विधुर *n.* Alarm, agitation. **विधुरदर्शन** *n.* The experiencing or feeling of alarm.

विधेय *fut. pass. part.* To be done. (*rt.* **धा**, Hold.)

विना *ind.* Without; *governing acc. or ins.*

विनीति *f.* Homage.

विनोदेन *ins. sin. of* **विनोद** *m.* Diversion, entertainment.

विप्रलब्ध *pass. part.* Deceived. (*rt.* **लभ्**, Gain.)

विमर्द *m.* Destroying, breaking.

विमृश्य, Having considered, pondered. (*rt.* **मृश्.**)

वियति *loc. sin. of* **वियत्** *n.* Air, sky.

विलपन *n.* Lamentation, complaint. **विलप्य** *ind. pret. part of* **लप** *1st cl. par. with* **वि**, Lament.

विलम्ब *m.* Delay.

विलिप्त, Besmeared. (*rt.* **लिप**, Smear.)

विलोक्य, Having observed. (*rt.* **लोक** *10th cl. par.* See, look.)

विवर *n.* A hole or burrow, a mouse-hole.

विवाह *m.* A marriage. **विवाहचतुष्टय** *n.* TATP. A quarternion of marriages, four marriages.

विशाल, Great, large.

विशिष्ट, Distinguished, excellent. **विशिष्टवर्ण** BAHUV. Of a distinguished or choice colour.

विश्वास *m.* Trust, confidence. **विश्वास्य**, Having inspired with confidence. *ind. pret. part. of caus. of* **श्वस**, Breathe,—*with* **वि**, Believe.

विषण्ण, Downcast. (*rt.* **षद्**, Sink.)

विषय *m.* An object of sense; department, sphere.

विषाद *m.* Dejection, grief.

विषीदत *2d pl. imp. rt.* **षद्** *1st cl. par.* Sink, *with* **वि**, Despond.

विषुवत् *n.* The equinox. **विषुवत्सङ्क्रान्ति** *f.* TATP. The passage of the sun to the next sign at the equinoxes.

विष्णुशर्म्मा *nom. sin. of* **विष्णुशर्म्मन्** *m.* A proper name.

विसर्पन् *nom. sin. pres. part.* (No. 125. *rt.* **सृप** *1st cl. par.* Go, move), Gliding. (Obs. *In extract* 3, p. 49, *in the expression* **विसर्पँस्तांस्तङ्कुलकयान्**, *the letter* **स्** *is twice interposed, for the sake of euphony, between the nasal and the* **त** *following.*)

विस्तीर्ण *pass. part.* Spread, stretched, strewed. (*rt.* **स्तॄ**, Spread.)

विस्मित, Surprised. (*rt.* **स्मि**, Smile.)

विहस्य, Having laughed. (*rt.* **हस**, Laugh.)

विहार *m.* A roaming about for pleasure; a temporary building for festal purposes.

वृक्ष *m.* A tree. **वृक्षाग्र** *n.* The top of a tree.

वृत्त *pass. part.* (*rt.* **वृत**), Done happened. *s. n.* A livelihood; behaviour.

वृद्ध, Old.

वृषभ *m.* A bull.

वृष्टि *f.* Rain, wet weather.

वेला *f.* Time.

व्यवस्थाप्य, Having set or placed. (*rt.* **स्था**, Stand.)

व्यवहार *m.* Behaviour; the practice of the law-courts.

व्यसन *n.* Calamity, vice.

व्याकुल, Bewildered.

व्याघ्र, A tiger.

व्याध, A hunter.

व्यापादित, Slain. *pass. part. caus.* (*rt.* **पद**, Go, *with* **आ** *and* **वि**) **व्यापादितवान्** *nom. sin. m. indef. part. part.* He killed.

व्यापार *m.* Effort, exercise, business, profession; a meddling.

श *śa.*

शकट *n.* A cart.

शक्तु *m.* or *n.* Flour, meal.

शक्य *fut. pass. part. of* **शक** *5th cl. par,* Be able. *The passive form of this verb gives to an associated infinitive mood a passive sense.*

शठ, Knavish.

शत *n.* A hundred.

शनैस् (*or* **शनैः शनैस्**) *ind.* Slowly, softly, gently. Now and then.

शपथ *m.* An oath.

शब्द *m.* A sound, noise, cry.

शर *m.* An arrow.

शरण *n.* An asylum.

शराव *m.* A dish or platter.

शशक, A hare.

शान्त, Abated.

शाल्मली *f.* The silk cotton tree.

शास्त्र *n.* An order or command. Scripture, science; institutes of religion, law, letters, &c.

शिखर *m.* or *n.* A peak, summit of a mountain.

शिव *adj.* Prosperous.

शिशु *m.* a child. **शिशोः** *gen. sin.*

शीत, Cold. **शीतार्त्त** TATP. Pained by the cold.

शुश्राव, He heard (No. 57).

शूकर *m.* A boar.

शृणु, Hearken. (*rt.* **श्रु** *irreg.* See No. 38.)

शैथिल्य *n.* Remissness.

शैल *m.* A mountain. **शैलशिखर** *m.* or *n.* TATP. A mountain-peak.

श्रवण *n.* Hearing.

श्राद्ध *n.* A funeral ceremony.

श्रीपर्वत *m.* Name of a mountain, or range of mountains.

श्रीमत् *adj.* Illustrious. श्रीमद्देवपादाः *nom. pl. m.* TATP. The feet of your glorious majesty.

श्रुत, Heard. (*rt.* श्रु, No. 38.)

श्रूयते, It is heard. श्रूयताम्, Let it be heard. (*rt.* श्रु, Hear; Nos. 91 and 132.) श्रोतुम्, To hear. (No. 124.)

श्लोकः *m.* A stanza.

श्वा *nom. sin. of* श्वन्, A dog. श्वानम् *acc.*

स *sa.*

स *A contraction of* सह, With, *often appears as the first member of an* AVYA. *and a* BAHUV. *compound.* (*See further, under* सः.)

संयुक्त, Possessed of. (*rt.* युज, Join.)

संवर्धयति, Causes to thrive. (वर्द्धि *caus. of* वृध, Increase, *with* सम्, No. 130.)

संशय *m.* Doubt.

संस्थाप्य, Having appointed.

सः *nom. sin. m. of* तद्, No. 81, He (she, it, or that). *The visarga drops before a consonant,* No. 88.

सकल, All.

सकाशम् *ind.* Near.

सकोप BAHUV. Angry (*See* स). सकोपम् AVYA. Angrily.

सखे *voc. sin. of* सखि, A friend.

सङ्ख्यक (*Terminational adjective*), Numbering, amounting to.

सङ्ग्राम *m.* War, battle.

सचकितम् AVYA. Timidly.

सञ्चरन्ति, They rove or prowl about. (*rt.* चर 1*st cl. par.*) सञ्चरन् *nom. sin. m. pres. part.*

सञ्चिन्त्य, Having maturely considered.

सञ्जातेर्ष्याः *nom. pl. f.* BAHUV. Grown envious.

सञ्जीवकनन्दकनामानौ *acc. du. m.* BAHUV. Named Sanjívaka and Nandaka(—a certain pair of bullocks).

सत् *part. pres. of* अस, Be. सति *ins. sin. m.* or *n.*

सततम् *ind.* Always, continually.

सत्वरम् AVYA. Quickly.

सनाथीक्रियताम्, Let it be made to possess a master.

सन्तति *f.* Offspring.

सन्तु, Let them be. (*rt.* अस 2*d cl. par.*)

सन्तुष्ट, Pleased. (*rt.* तुष, Be pleased.) *caus.* सन्तोष्य, Having gratified.

सन्दर्श्य *caus.* Having shown. (*rt.* दृश, See.)

सन्धान *n.* A holding together, an alliance.

सन्ध्या *f.* The twilight. सन्ध्यासमय *m.* Eventide.

सन्निधान *n.* Proximity.

सपत्नी, A rival wife. **सपत्न्यः** *nom. pl.*

सभयम् AVYA. With fear, timidly.

समधिक *adj.* Exceeding, abundant.

समर्थ, Able.

समायात, Arrived, come. (*rt.* **या**, Go.) (*See* No. 130.)

समावासित *adj.* Taking up a residence. **समवासितकटक** BAHUV. Encamped. —(*i.e.* whose camp has taken up a location).

समीप, Near.

समुपस्थित, Arrived, impending.

समृद्ध, Prosperous, affluent. (*rt.* **ऋध**, Prosper.)

सम्प्रति, Now.

सम्भवति, It is possible. (*rt.* **भू**, Be.)

सम्भाव्य, Having thought possible, or surmised.

सम्मत *n.* Consent, approval, opinion.

सरः *nom.* or *acc. of* **सरस्**, A lake or pond. **सरस्तीरे**, On the margin of a lake.

सर्प, A serpent.

सर्व्व, *pronominal*, All, every.

सर्व्वदा, Always.

सर्वस्वामिगुणोपेत, Possessing all lordly excellences.

सविशेषम् *ind.* In an especial manner.

ससर्प BAHUV. With a serpent, infested by serpents.

सह *ind. governing the ins. case,* With, along with.

सहज *adj.* Innate, natural.

सहसा *ind.* Quickly, precipitately.

साधयामि, I accomplish, kill. *rt.* **साध** 10*th cl. par.* **साधयन्ति** 3*d pl.* **साधयितव्य** *fut. part. pass.* **साधित** *pass. part.*

सान्निध्य *n.* Nearness, close attendance.

सार *m.* Sum, amount.

सार्द्धम् *ind.* With, along with; *governing ins. case.*

साष्टाङ्गपातम् AVYA. With a prostration of the eight members. *See* **अष्टाङ्गपात**.

सिंह *m.* A lion.

सुख *n.* Pleasure, happiness.

सुखोपविष्टाणाम् TATP. *gen. pl.* Seated comfortably, or at ease. *See* **उपविष्ट**.

सुत *m.* A son. **सुतनिर्विशेष**, Precisely as one's own son (—without distinction from a son).

सुदर्शन *adj.* Good-looking, well-discerning.

सुदूर, Very distant.

सुप्त *pass. part.* Asleep. Lying down. (*rt.* **स्वप्** Sleep.)

सुवर्ण *n.* Gold. **सुवर्णवती** *f.* Name of a city. (Possessing gold).

सुस्थ *agt.* Happy. Safe and sound.

सुहृत्तमाः *nom. pl. m.* (*superl. of* **सुहृद्**, A friend), Most affectionate, very friendly.

सुहृद् *m.* A friend. **सुहृद्भेद** *m.* TATP. A separation of friends.

सेवा *f.* Service.

सोढ *past. part.* Endured, put up with (*rt.* सह्).

स्थल *n.* A place, spot, soil, dry or firm ground.

स्थातुम् *inf.* To stand. (*rt.* स्था.)

स्थान *n.* A place, station. A staying.

स्थास्यसि, Thou shalt stand. 2*d fut.* *of* स्था (No. 38). स्थित *pass. part.* स्थित्वा *ind. pret. part.*

स्थेय *m.* A judge, arbiter. स्थेयाभ्याम् *ins. du.*

स्नाति, He bathes. (*rt.* स्ना 2*d cl. par.*) स्नात *past. part. pass.*

स्नायु *f.* A sinew, tendon. स्नायुबन्धन *n.* Tatp. A sinew-string.

स्नेह *m.* Affection, friendship.

स्म *A particle imparting to the present tense a past signification.*

स्व *pronoun,* Own.

स्वपिति, He sleeps. (*rt.* स्वप 2*d cl. par. irreg.*)

स्वभाव *m.* Nature, natural property or disposition.

स्वयम् *ind.* Of one's self, of one's own accord. स्वयङ्कृत Tatp. Done by one's self.

स्वेच्छा *f.* One's own will, pleasure or choice. (स्व, Own, इच्छा, Wish). स्वेच्छाहारविहार *m.* A feeding and roaming about according to one's inclination.

ह *ha.*

हंस *m.* A goose, a swan.

हत *pass. part.* Smitten, wounded, slain. (*rt.* हन 2*d cl. par.*) हत्वा *ind. pret. part.* हनिष्यसि 2*d sin.* 2*d fut.* हन्तव्य *fut. pass. part.*

हरति 3*d sin. pres. of* हृ, Carry off. हर्तुम् *inf.*

हस्त *m.* A hand, a paw, an elephant's trunk.

हस्ती *nom. sin. of* हस्तिन् *m.* An elephant.

हृदि *loc. sin. of* हृद् *n.* The heart. The mind, or seat of thought.

हृष्टपुष्टाङ्ग Bahuv. Frisky and fat. (हृष्ट, Pleased, पुष्ट, Fed, *and* अङ्ग, Body.)

हेतु *m.* A cause, reason. हेतोः *abl.* or *gen.* On account of, by reason of.

SUGGESTIONS IN REGARD TO AN ELEMENTARY COURSE OF SANSKRIT STUDY.

THESE "First Lessons" having been gone through, and having given the student (it is to be hoped) a taste for this noblest of languages, some suggestions in regard to his further prosecution of the study may not be unacceptable.

If the student desires merely to pass the Civil Service examination, for India, his best plan is, of course, to adhere closely to whatever may be prescribed in the annually issued instructions of the Civil Service Commissioners for the time being. But, over and above this, some students at least, among those who seek an Indian career, may aspire to become more fully acquainted with that language and literature which, as being the pride of the people of India, may conceivably furnish the key to their hearts. The following suggestions apply to both of the supposed classes, to some extent,—but more especially to the latter.

Instead of taking up Wilson's Grammar, and Johnson's *Hitopadeśa,* after reading the prose extracts from the *Hitopadeśa* included in this brochure, let the student, if only for a change of style, take up the "Story of Nala", as edited by Professor Monier Williams, of Oxford. In this edition he will have the aid of the beautiful, and remarkably close, poetical version by Dean Milman,—which does not, however, give more than an allowable amount of aid to the beginner whose great aim is to acquire a *copia verborum.* In the analytical vocabulary, arranged on a plan similar to that of the vocabulary in these "First Lessons", the references to grammatical rules presuppose the possession of Professor Williams's grammar. This grammar, though not so full as that of Wilson, is in several respects better calculated to win the attention of the student,—especially the classical student. The study of it may advantageously precede that of Wilson's grammar, provided that the pupil destined for India shall guard against being led away by the author's ingenious, eloquent, and (—I had almost said—) insidious disparagement of the native Hindú methods of tuition. On that point it would not do to dwell here;—I only beg the student at all events to suspend his judgment—till he can judge for himself.

While going through the *Nala*, the student may profitably engage himself upon the exercises (for translation into Sanskrit) contained in Professor Williams's little Sanskrit "Manual". If studying by himself, he will here scarcely be able to dispense with the same author's "Dictionary, English and Sanskrit".

Having finished the *Nala*, he may profitably take up Professor Johnson's complete edition of the *Hitopadeśa*; studying at the same time Wilson's grammar, with the omission, in the first instance, of the portions the omission of which is noticed, in the latest instructions issued by the Commissioners, as permissible or advisable.

As Wilson's Sanskrit dictionary is unhappily out of print (—though that of Yates may form a meagre substitute—), the analytical vocabularies attached to the books just mentioned are a great boon to the student. The famous poem—the *Meghadúta*, or "Messenger-Cloud",—has been edited with similar apparatus by Professor Johnson; but the student (—unless he be fond of logic—) had better relegate this to a considerably later stage in his progress; for the compound words, though exquisitely constructed, are of merciless length, and demand a tension of the mind which is not pleasing to all,—nor at every time to any. The accompanying versified English version by Professor Wilson is assuredly not more than a legitimate help to the student,—under which aspect alone, as mentioned in the preface, the Professor allowed his version to accompany the text. The "Selections from the Mahábhárata", by Professor Johnson, (edited much like his *Hitopadeśa*, yet with some further call for exertion on the part of the student,) may profitably intervene between the reading of the *Hitopadeśa* and the *Megha-dúta*.

Supposing us (—pupil and teacher—) to have got thus far, I have nothing that I now incline to suggest to the home students of Sanskrit, who will find indicated to them, in the catalogues of Bonn, Berlin, and St. Petersburgh,—or more compactly in that of Messrs. Williams and Norgate (London)—a considerable amount of pabulum (—in the convenient shape of texts with Latin versions—) for the lover of this language. But if the Indian Civil servant wishes to gain the ear, and influence the mind, of the leaders of Hindú thought—the learned Bráhmans—he must go through a course of reading more dry, and to many minds (—with whom I do not here quite sympathize—) more repulsive than that which has been hitherto spoken of. Grammar and metaphysics are the delight of the learned Hindú (—whom all other Hindús look up to—), and if you wish to reach his heart, you will do well to obtain some acquaintance with his philosophy and his grammar in the very shape in which he himself possesses them and treasures them.

It is a great mistake to suppose that the marvellously condensed grammar of PÁṆINI (the chief of Sanskrit grammarians) is designedly obscure. The charge of intentional obscurity might with equal reason be brought against the Binomial Theorem, which Newton assuredly never intended as an enigma. To take a simpler illustration:—think how hard it is to carry in one's memory the arithmetical rule for the extraction of the cube-root, or even of the square root. Yet how easy it is to remember the algebraical formula $(a + b) \times (a + b) = a^2 + 2\,ab + b^2$, from which the rule for the extraction of the square root may at any time be re-derived with perfect certainty. Analogously:—it is not very easy to remember, with full confidence, the specification in regard to the rule for the change of the dental *n* to the cerebral, after *ṛi*, *r*, or *sh*,—viz. (as Professor Williams neatly puts it*) "even though क *k*, ग *g*, प *p*, ब *b*, (or their aspirates,) ह *h*, य *y*, व *v*, or म *m*, intervene":—and further, if there chance at any time to be a dispute as to which are the letters in question, it can be settled only by turning to some volume,—which may happen not to be at hand. But how easy it is for the Hindú to remember the formula of PÁṆINI, viz., अट्कुप्वाङ्नुम्व्यवायेऽपि,—like the "Propria quæ maribus" of our fathers:—and such an appeal to the memoria technica decides the question (—without book—) both for one's self and for others competent to have an opinion.

It would be out of place here to go much farther into the question of the native Hindú system of grammar, but I feel bound to state, briefly, that the apparently prevalent notion in regard to the order of the studies of a young *Bráhmaṇ*, is incorrect,—and mischievously

* With intentional omission, I conjecture, of the mention of the vowels and diphthongs,—as tending to cumber the rule with precautions and provisos—necessary in the case of the logical-minded Hindú, but not so indispensable in the case of the looser, rough and ready, intellect of Englishmen in general.

incorrect. I feel the more bound to mention this briefly (—reserving a fuller explanation for a possibly future occasion—) because I myself, in the Preface to the English version of the *Laghu Kaumudí* (published at Benares in 1849) re-echoed, in some measure, the erroneous tradition still too prevalent. Well then, — it is *true* that a Hindú student requires at least ten years to become perfectly proficient throughout the whole range of the grammatical literature of the Sanskrit;—but it is an erroneous inference that he studies nothing else during the ten years required for his becoming thus thoroughly proficient. Whilst he is committing to memory the condensed aphorisms of PÁṆINI, (without explanation at the time,) he is not only reading quantities of poetry which his teacher explains to him in the vernacular, but he is learning paradigms of nouns and verbs,—"*Râmah, Rámau, Rámáh, iti prathamá*; *Rámam, Rámau, Rámán, iti dwitíyá*;" and so on. He learns the *Páṇiníyan* grammar with the view of being able, as regards the Sanskrit grammar, to render at any time (—to himself in the first instance—) a reason for the faith that is in him. As I am here mainly concerned about preventing the student (—intended for India—) from imbibing an unjustifiable and mischievous prejudice against the native Hindú expositions of grammar and philosophy, I dwell rather upon the imputations which have been cast upon these Hindú systems, than upon the merited commendation bestowed upon them by Professor Wilson, for example, who declared that the *Páṇiníyan* grammar must be studied by every one who desired to learn Sanskrit "thoroughly and in earnest",—and who added afterwards that the aphorisms of PÁṆINI (—usually spoken of, after Sir William Jones, as being "dark as the darkest oracle"—) are—since the issue of the English version of the *Laghu Kaumudí*—"now quite clear".

With regard to Hindú Philosophy, the learner may advisably, at first, view it, broadly, under three phases,—viz. (1) The Philosophy of the Sage GAUTAMA (—termed the *Nyáya* Philosophy—), (2) that of the Sage KAPILA (—termed the *Sánkhya* Philosophy—), and (3) that of the Sage BÁDARÁYAṆA (—termed the *Vedánta* Philosophy). These systems are, all three, studied by Indian students,—generally in the order in which they have been just enumerated. Though they differ noticeably from one another, yet they are held to be not irreconcileable, because, in seeking to give a comprehensive exposition of the totality of things, it is in their *point of view* that they differ most. They may be described (—as I have remarked elsewhere*—) as severally regarding the Universe as it stands in relation severally to Sensation, Emotion, and Intellection. The school of the *Nyáya*, founding on the fact that we have various, and seemingly heterogeneous, sensations, inquires what, and how many, are the channels through which such varied knowledge flows in. Finding that there are five very different channels, five different externals, adapted to these, are inferred. Hence the Indian theory of the "Five Elements",—not of four as in Ancient Europe. The simplest introduction to the *Nyáya* system is the little manual called the *Tarka Sangraha*, the text of which, with an English translation and commentary, has been printed for the use of the Benares College. This manual includes, under one of its topics, an exposition of the Hindú terms of Logic, and of the systematic forms in which arguments are propounded or assailed by the learned of India. These deserve especial attention, on the part of the student who is going to India,—inasmuch as a familiarity with them will save a great deal of trouble, and of probably unfortunate misunderstanding on both sides, when he enters on any serious reasoning with a Hindú philosopher.

As the beginner (—for whom these suggestions are intended—) has had perhaps enough (—or what he may, not improbably, consider more than enough—) of these disquisitions, I here break off,—only advising the student to suspend his judgment in regard to the Hindú systems till he shall have examined them.

* Christianity contrasted with Hindú Philosophy, p. xvii.

PRINTED BY BALLANTYNE, HANSON AND CO.
EDINBURGH AND LONDON.